STUDYING *The Sixth Sense*

Mark Kirwan-Hayhoe

Contents

Factsheet

The Sixth Sense ....1999, USA

Running Time ....107 mins, 24 secs

Certificate ....PG-13 (USA), 15 (UK)

Production Companies ....Hollywood Pictures, Spyglass Entertainment, The Kennedy/Marshall Company

Distributor.............................Buena Vista (USA), Buena Vista International (UK)

Budget ....$40 million.

Release Dates and Strategies ..Released on 2,161 screens on 6 August 1999 in the USA (premiered in Philadelphia on 2 August) and 9 screens on 7 November 1999 in the UK.

Key credits

Director ....M. Night Shyamalan

Producers ....Kathleen Kennedy, Frank Marshall and Barry Mendel

Screenplay..............................M. Night Shyamalan

Director of Photography ....Tak Fujimoto

Editor.....................................Andrew Mondshein

Production Designer ....Larry Fulton

Music.....................................James Newton Howard

Cast

Malcolm Crowe ....Bruce Willis

Cole Sear ....Haley Joel Osment

Lynn Sear...............................Toni Collette

Anna Crowe...........................Olivia Williams

Vincent Gray ....Donnie Wahlberg

Sean ....Glenn Fitzgerald

Kyra Collins...........................Mischa Barton

Synopsis

Malcolm Crowe and his wife Anna are celebrating a citation from the mayor of Philadelphia for his work as a child psychologist when Vincent Gray, a former patient, breaks into their home. Vincent blames Malcolm for failing to help him when he was younger, then shoots Malcolm before killing himself. The next Fall, Malcolm takes on the case of Cole Sear, a disturbed nine-year-old who lives with his mother Lynn. While working with the boy, Malcolm is worried his marriage is collapsing and that his wife may be contemplating an affair with a younger man. After Malcolm tells Cole why he is sad in the form of a bedtime story, Cole finally reveals his secret of being visited by dead people. Listening to a taped session with Vincent, Malcolm becomes convinced Cole is telling the truth and suggests the ghosts are trying to communicate with him. Kyra, a girl who died mysteriously, leads Cole to a box containing a videotape that proves she was murdered, which is seen by guests at her funeral. Cole appears in a school play and is cheered by his schoolmates, who previously ostracised him. He then tells his mother about his 'gift' and she believes him after he delivers a message from her own dead mother. Cole and Malcolm agree there is no longer any need for therapy. Malcolm goes home and discovers his wife still loves him, but that he did not survive the shooting.

1. Introduction

The Sixth Sense (1999), directed by M. Night Shyamalan and starring Bruce Willis and Haley Joel Osment, has become something of a contemporary legend for the aspiring scriptwriter/film-maker. The story goes like this. M. Night Shyamalan (pronounced *Shah*-ma-lawn), a young, unknown film school graduate, predicts the next script he writes will sell for $2 million and star Bruce Willis. When the screenplay is offered for auction, it actually sells for $3 million in less than a day – the highest amount ever paid for a first time script. The writer has also been signed on to direct his feature film debut and, shortly after, Bruce Willis agrees to play the lead. When the film is released, it becomes the sleeper hit of the year and one of the biggest grossing films of all time.

Fig. 1: Night and camera
(© Moviestore Collection)

Well, not quite.

Like most legends, it is based on truth, but there is also a great deal of embellishment. Shyamalan was not an unknown film school graduate, but a professional already making a living in the film industry; he was not a first time scriptwriter; he did not receive $3 million for the screenplay and it was not the highest amount ever paid for a script, first or otherwise;[1] he was not a first time director – and, despite the repeated assertion even in the trade papers on both sides of the Atlantic, *The Sixth Sense* was not a sleeper hit.

As is often the case in Hollywood, the actual story is more remarkable, but less gripping.

Manoj Nelliyattu Shyamalan (the name Night, by which he is known professionally, he thought up while attending college) was born in Pondicherry, India in 1970.[2] He grew up in Philadelphia and attended a variety of Catholic schools, to which he was sent for the strict discipline. He was the only Indian in attendance and was brought up a Hindu at home. At the age of 8 (or 10 or 12, depending on which biographical article you read) he was given a

Super-8 camera and by the time he was 16 (or 17) he had produced 45 short films. Initially intending to be a doctor – both his parents are physicians – he soon gave up this career path and instead focused on his passion for film-making, attending New York University's Tisch School of the Arts. Upon graduating, he set about raising money for what he hoped would be his first film, *Wide Awake*. However, when the financing collapsed, he wrote *Praying With Anger* (1992), a story about an Indian-American sent to an Indian university for a year. Using the remaining funds from *Wide Awake*, Shyamalan found some new investors, flew to India and shot the film for $750,000. As well as writing it, the 22-year-old also produced, directed and starred in it. *Praying With Anger* won the American Film Institute's debut film competition in 1993, but commercially it had virtually no return due to its very limited, or rather non-existent, exhibition release (though it did eventually recoup its investment).

After *Praying With Anger*, the independent production company Miramax – at that time riding high on their Tarantino double whammy of *Reservoir Dogs* (1992) and *Pulp Fiction* (1994), as well as distribution successes such as

---

NOTES:

1 However, he did achieve this with his next script *Unbreakable* (2000), for which Disney paid $5 million.

2 His parents, Jayalakshmi and Nelliate, went there specifically to give birth to him.

Introduction

The Crying Game (1992) – agreed to finance *Wide Awake*. However, not only did the film get stuck in post-production for almost two years (while Shyamalan argued with the production company about the tone of the final cut), but when it was finally released in 1998, it was one of the year's lowest grossing movies, with a return of only $258,212. Shyamalan thus joined the list of eminent directors whose first mainstream feature films were box-office failures (Steven Spielberg, George Lucas, Oliver Stone et al).[3] During this period, he scripted *Labour of Love*, which he sold to Twentieth Century Fox.[4] Then, in 1997, he adapted E. B. White's classic children's novel *Stuart Little* (1999) for Columbia during the day and worked on *The Sixth Sense* at night, which he sold to Hollywood Pictures (a subsidiary of Disney Studios) for $2.5 million upfront versus $500,000 deferred – gaining a total of $3 million for writing *and* directing services.

However, what is far more remarkable is the deal itself. Not only was *The Sixth Sense* sold in less than 24 hours of being put up for auction as a result of a bidding frenzy between four major production companies (uncommon, but not unheard of), but the deal included a highly unusual clause of a 'writer's final cut', which guaranteed the script would be given a 'greenlight' without a demand for at least one rewrite.

A spec script is a screenplay that has not been developed by a studio or production company. In other words, it has been written independently of any deal and offered on the open market. To greenlight a picture is to agree the screenplay is ready to be filmed essentially as it has been written. Before a studio commits its finances to a multi-million dollar film, it understandably wants to make sure that the final script is as good as it can be (though sometimes it results in exactly the opposite). As such, script development is usually a slow, laborious business involving numerous rewrites before the greenlight is given. For a spec script to be greenlighted as is, without changes being requested, shows a level of commitment and belief in the project on the part of the production company – not to mention the level of skill on the part of the writer – that is rare, to say the least. In fact, there seems to have been no other example of this kind of deal in contemporary Hollywood. The nearest comparable instance did not even have a script, just a treatment. That film was Michael Cimino's *Heaven's Gate* (1980). It was magnificent, multi-layered, uncompromising, visually stunning, superbly acted and directed by someone touched with the genius of perfection. It was also one of the biggest box-office disasters ever made and destroyed United Artists as an autonomous institution.[5]

Clearly, Hollywood Pictures had enormous confidence in the script, for they were certainly willing to take considerable risks in regards to other major aspects of the film. Shyamalan's proven track record at that time as a director was one film, one flop (it would shortly be two for two, but fortunately *The Sixth Sense* deal was made before *Wide Awake* was released). Though Willis had previously proven himself to be a thoughtful actor in films such as *In Country* (1989) and *Twelve Monkeys* (1995), commercially audiences clearly preferred him in the role of action hero. Not only that, but Willis's previous outing with a child actor (who coincidentally also played a boy who was 'special') – *Mercury Rising* (1998) – had been both a critical and box-office failure. Furthermore, there were going to be no obvious special effects and the pace of the film was incredibly slow compared to standard Hollywood studio fare. Finally, though there was no explosive action sequences, female nudity or on-screen violence – and as such would not be as appealing to the biggest demographic audience, 15 to 24-year-old males – it clearly contained moments of horror, which meant the lowest classification rating it was going to get was an PG-13 (which it received), thus losing the substantial kiddie market.[6]

In fact, this uncertain target audience, combined

NOTES:

3 It is sometimes erroneously cited that *Duel* (1971) is Spielberg's first film. In fact, *Duel* was made for television, but its success in this format in the U.S. led to it being released as a feature internationally after further editing and some additional footage. Spielberg's actual cinematic debut is *The Sugarland Express* (1974).

4 It has still to go into production.

5 For the full inside story regarding Hollywood's greatest folly since D. W. Griffith's *Intolerance* (1916), read Stephen Bach's *Final Cut: Dreams and Disaster in the making of Heaven's Gate*, Jonathan Cape Ltd., 1985.

6 In Britain, it received a 15 certificate.

with the film's mix of genres, resulted in the marketing division being somewhat bewildered in terms of how to sell the film. There are hints that Hollywood Pictures were aware of this, but felt the resulting film could succeed despite the potential problems of promotion and publicity. What none of them could have known, however, was just weeks before *The Sixth Sense*'s release date, a 'no-budget' horror film would appear that would take gargantuan box-office and the whole of the Hollywood industry by surprise. The success of *The Blair Witch Project* (1999) left no one in any doubt that it was not merely the horror film of the year, but of the decade. As a consequence, the promotional run-up to *The Sixth Sense*'s release was somewhat lacklustre. In fact, the marketing division had such little faith in it they did not even bother to push for its inclusion in *Entertainment Weekly*'s 1999 Summer Movie Previews – a list of 134 films that even included such potential blockbusters (sic) as *Universal Soldier: The Return*.

Theatrical trailers for the film emphasised the ghostly subject matter, built around the tag line 'I see dead people' rather than the star, despite Willis's recent highly successful (and equally ludicrous) *Armageddon* (1998), also for Disney. The television spots were not even that focused. They made a vague attempt to sell it as an old-school horror film, but old-school horror was not in vogue after *The Blair Witch Project*. Essentially, Disney thought the ship had sailed.

The Sixth Sense was the second biggest grossing film of the year, after *Star Wars Episode I: The Phantom Menace* (1999). It grossed over $275 million in the 24 weeks it remained in North America's domestic Top 30 and over $660 million worldwide, making it at one point the ninth biggest film of all time in terms of box office receipts. As of this time of writing (2005), it is still in the top 20.

There are a number of reasons why *The Sixth Sense* is worthy of study. Its approach to narrative and use of genre show an understanding of Hollywood film-making

conventions, which at the same time both develops and subverts those conventions. Its characterisation, development of themes and stylistic approaches are subtle, meticulous and, when related to Shyamalan's previous and subsequent films, show a consistency which brings to mind that somewhat obsolete (and certainly overused) idea of auteurism. However, if for no other reason, *The Sixth Sense* is worth studying for one aspect alone. It is a quintessential example of a film not only deliberately going against conventional Hollywood wisdom and succeeding in spectacular fashion, but one that achieves this despite all the odds seemingly against it. In so doing, it proved yet again scriptwriter William Goldman's famous and oft-quoted adage that in the movie business, 'nobody knows anything'.[7]

NOTES:

7 Goldman, *Adventures In The Screen Trade*, 1983.

1. Narrative (and Genre)

On initial viewing, the narrative of *The Sixth Sense* appears simplistic. A child psychologist who failed to help one patient is given a 'second chance' – another boy who seems to be suffering from the same condition. In doing so, both the psychologist and the boy successfully face their fears and move on in their lives (sic). These events are told in chronological order throughout the film, with the exception of the final sequence in which a series of flashbacks occur that the audience have already seen, but now reinterpret in the light of new information they were unaware of previously, a sequence early on in the film in which we see events that have occurred in the past while hearing dialogue spoken at the film's current point in time and a very brief flashback approximately two-thirds of the way through.

Appearances are deceptive – and in the case of this film, appearances are extremely deceptive. What seems to be a relatively straightforward tale (albeit one with a highly unusual twist at the end) told in a relatively straightforward way is in fact neither. The story of *The Sixth Sense* will be explored in more depth in both sections Two and Three. However, before the specifics of *The Sixth Sense*'s narrative can be approached, certain key concepts need to be considered.

Narrative: An Overview

The differences between story, plot and narrative are relatively simple to understand, but notoriously difficult to explain. Essentially, the **story** is the events that occur within a film in chronological order *and* events that can be inferred from the film, but do not appear in it; the **plot** is the order in which the events seen on screen appear in the telling of the story; the **narrative** is the way in which these events are presented to the audience.

Citizen Kane (1941) is an excellent example that shows the differences between narrative, story and plot. The story is about the life and death of the phenomenally wealthy Charles Foster Kane. Some of the events in Kane's life are seen on screen, some are not (for example, we do not see any of Kane's upbringing under the guardianship of Thatcher, but we can clearly infer it was not a happy one). The plot tells the story of his life from various points of view, but in a non-sequential order (for example, the first event the audience sees is Kane's death). The narrative lets the audience know more about the events surrounding Kane's life and death than any single character in the film knows, including Kane himself. (for example, it gives us – on a surface level – not only the answer to the question of what 'Rosebud' is, the device that drives the film forward, but also what happens to it. No character in the film is aware of both these pieces of information). In other words, the narrative is **omniscient**; it gives us more information than any one character is aware of. The opposite of this is **restricted** narrative, which is when the audience experiences no more than (invariably) the lead character in a film does at any time. In other words, we see and hear exactly what that character sees and hears at the same point in the film's progression.[8]

To give a simple example: a film with restricted narrative shows our hero/ine watch a man run into a house, which then explodes. S/he runs across to the house and sees an unrecognisable body in the remains. At this point, our hero/ine could think the body is that of the man or somebody else, exactly as we, the audience could think. Neither the character nor the audience at that point knows if it is the man. However, if the film cuts to inside the house after the man runs into it, and then shows him either being killed or escaping, setting up the explosion or unintentionally triggering it, at this point we, the audience know more than our hero/ine. This is omniscient narrative.

NOTES:

8 An extreme example of this is *The Lady In The Lake* (1947), in which the audience experiences the entire film through the 'eyes' of the lead character, i.e. the camera.

The reason why narrative and plot are frequently thought to be one and the same thing is that often in Hollywood films they *are* the same thing. This is because the most popular form of storytelling in Hollywood – and film around the world – is **classical Hollywood narrative**.

Classical Hollywood narrative is a form of film-making in which the story, and the events within the story, is presented in a linear fashion. Events occur sequentially, one following another in a cause and effect chain. In other words, there is a logic to the order of the events as we see them in terms of time and space. Films that use the classical Hollywood narrative mode of storytelling do not suddenly jump forwards and backwards in time, such as can be seen in *Pulp Fiction*, where a character is killed, only to reappear in the film later in terms of screen duration, but earlier in terms of the narrative's temporal events. The fact the character reappears is not a break from classical Hollywood narration per se; it is that the character reappears without any signification that the narrative has moved back in time. The audience is not directly informed of this temporal change; we have to work it out for ourselves. Similarly, classical Hollywood narrative does not attempt to show events in different spaces occurring simultaneously, such as can be seen in *Magnolia* (1999), which rapidly cuts from one event and place to another and another, or the original version of *The Thomas Crown Affair* (1968) or *Timecode* (2000), which show events in different places at the same time through varying uses of split-screen technology.

However, there is more to classical Hollywood narrative than simply a telling of the story in a logical, sequential form. Firstly, classical Hollywood narrative is character driven. The characters – or **protagonists** – are almost always the agents of the story; in other words, they create the cause and effect chain that moves the story onwards. Even when there is a non-human agent in the story (for example, the large meteorite heading towards Earth in the previously-mentioned *Armageddon*), the narrative is driven by how the protagonists deal with this non-human agent; the decisions they make, the actions they take determine the story's direction. In doing this, the characters inform us of 'what makes them tick'. They reveal their strengths and weaknesses, their aspirations and their vulnerabilities. The importance of this is that, by relating to the protagonists, the audience becomes interested in their plight. If we do not care about the characters, we do not care about what happens to them and the film fails as a piece of storytelling. In classical Hollywood narrative, this often also involves letting us know who we should align ourselves with by distinguishing between those we are meant to regard positively (the 'hero') and those we should regard negatively (the 'villain'). The entire storyline of *High Noon* (1952), for example, is built around an individual who decides to stand alone with the odds stacked against him.[9] We are meant to root for him, to admire his bravery and courage. If the narrative allowed us to empathise with those gunning for him, the film would collapse in terms of our engagement with the protagonist's predicament.

The distinguishing between positive and negative elements forms the basis of Claude Lévi-Strauss' narrative theory of 'binary oppositions'. Lévi-Strauss was as anthropologist who looked at common narrative structures in traditional stories across a range of societies and concluded that within all these stories lie the same basic 'myths' or cultural meanings that are explored through the use of 'binary oppositions' (pairs of opposites): life/death, civilisation/wilderness, rebellion/conformity, sacred/profane, etc. In other words, Lévi-Strauss suggests that all stories place opposites in conflict, and that each story is resolved with one of the binary opposites victorious over the other. In the case of film, by experiencing these oppositions through what is seen and heard on screen, the audience witness the resolution of conflicts that often cannot happen in the real world.

Secondly, classical Hollywood narrative is based on the idea of the three-act structure. This

---

NOTES:

9 Well, not totally alone. He has the love of a good woman who is able to fire a gun.

1. Narrative (and Genre)

approach has been employed since the early days of film-making, and was taken from the nineteenth-century stage melodramas so prominent when feature-length films first began to be produced. Film theorists refer to these 'acts' in a number of ways; for the purposes of this study, I shall refer to them as 'exposition', 'development' and 'resolution'.

Exposition is the part of the narrative that sets up the story events and the leading characters' traits and situations. In so doing, it creates a particular range of causes for what the audience sees on screen. In other words, it raises our expectations of what is to come in the film. An example of this is the opening scenes of **Psycho** (1960). In the first scene, we learn that office worker Marion Crane's lover Sam cannot afford to marry her due to his alimony payments. In the next, Marion's boss gives her a large sum of money to deposit into the bank. This is followed by a short scene of Marion packing a bag with the money still in her possession, then further scenes of her driving across country, intending to join Sam. This exposition has raised our expectations of what is to come in the film through a combination of the events that have occurred so far, the situation Marion finds herself in (in love with a man who professes to be too poor to marry her) and her character traits (one of which being that she finds it degrading having to meet him in hotel rooms at lunchtimes). At this point in the film there are any number of possible outcomes, but our expectations will revolve around two general alternatives: either Marion will be caught and punished or she will get away with the crime. The fact that Hitchcock later completely undermines our expectations is an example of how narrative can be developed in unexpected ways (see below).

In some cases, the exposition may refer to events and actions that occurred before the plot started. By doing this it allows the audience to connect events seen on screen with others not seen either directly or through inference. Most films do this to arouse curiosity or suspense. The plotting of **The Usual Suspects** (1995), for example, results

in the film opening on a series of actions that have already begun in order to create intrigue, in that it allows the audience to speculate on the possible causes of these actions. This type of opening is known as medias res (Latin for 'in the middle of things').

Development in classical Hollywood narrative has, as its basis, a continuous narrowing of cause and effect through the actions and reactions of the protagonist/s to the events surrounding them. As the plot proceeds, so the potential number of causes and effects that could occur decrease in number in readiness for the resolution. In other words, as the plot develops, the film will direct the audience towards a limited number of possible outcomes. The question then becomes which of these outcomes will occur or, alternatively, will the protagonist reach the desired outcome. However, narrative development does more than this. It can create audience expectations in respect to this outcome, and then delay it in terms of new obstacles (further actions that need to be undertaken by character to achieve the outcome), hidden obstacles (events or objects that could stop the character achieving the outcome, often resulting in audience suspense) or unexpected obstacles (events that delay the character achieving the outcome, often resulting in audience surprise). In essence, narrative development encourages us to form a long-term expectation it can then delay, subvert or fulfil. It can even undermine them entirely. To return to **Psycho**, Marion is indeed 'punished' – but not in the way the audience expected. Hitchcock kills her off and the film continues in an entirely different story direction.[10] In respect to plot development, then, the permutations are seemingly endless; however, these permutations tend to be variations of certain types of plot and as such exhibit certain patterns of narrative development.

As to how many of these 'basic' plots there are seems to have been debated almost as long as homo sapiens started telling the stories themselves. According to the Aristotle in his *Poetics*, there are four: simple fortunate, simple

---

NOTES:

10 This is one of the few successful examples of a film 'changing horses in mid-stream', something script gurus consistently warn against.

unfortunate, complex fortunate, complex unfortunate. Goethe thought there were seven. Georges Polti outlined thirty-six while Norman Friedman got it down to three – plots of fortune, of character and of thought. Unfortunately, he complicated things by stating that each plot had two possible endings, up or down (making it six); two possible protagonists, sympathetic or unsympathetic (twelve); and that there were six categories within plots of fortune, four within plots of character and four within plots of thought (you work it out). I give my students a guideline of three: rags-to-riches (actions by protagonist/s lead to eventual achievement of aim/s), selling-the-soul (actions by protagonist/s lead to eventual downfall) and surreal (not really sure who eventually got what or if there was anything to get).[11] While various independent, underground and European film-makers have used this last type, it never occurs in classical Hollywood narrative unless the plot is either (a) very bad or (b) *Being John Malkovich* (1999).

However, while it cannot be categorically stated as to exactly how many basic plots there are, classical Hollywood narrative does tend to favour two particular patterns of development. The first of these is a **change in knowledge**. This is where a protagonist discovers or learns something during the action that affects the subsequent action of the film. Usually, the character will learn several things, the most crucial being the final turning point of the film's development and which has an effect (either direct or indirect) on the film's climax.

The second pattern of development is **goal-oriented**. This is where the protagonist takes action to achieve either a desired object or a desired state. Goal-oriented plots tend to take one of two forms: the search or the investigation. In terms of the search, it does not matter if the thing being searched for is something particular (e.g. a person, a shark or an alien) or a general state of being (e.g. freedom, acceptance or love), as long as what is being searched for drives the narrative onward through a cause and effect manner. Similarly, the investigation is about the protagonist trying to discover information. This invariably involves the solving of some kind of mystery, but again it does not matter if the mystery revolves around an external thing (the microfilm, the missing person) or an internal one (the cause of nightmares, the reasons for schizophrenia). Sometimes, of course, there is both a search and an investigation.

Resolution is about endings and climaxes. Contrary to what is repeatedly written in introduction to film texts, some films do stop rather than end (John Sayles' *Limbo* (1999) being an example) – just not very many and certainly not Hollywood films.[12] Typically, a film using classical Hollywood narrative ends by narrowing the range of possible outcomes down to two very specific ones: success or failure by the protagonist/s in achieving the desired outcome/s. In doing so, it invariably also resolves any other causal issues or plot points that have been previously set up. The ending is therefore 'closed'; the chain of cause and effect is complete.[13] However, classical Hollywood narrative is more than just about a logically 'neat' ending where all the loose ends are tied up and presented to the audience one after the other.

To begin with, the resolution of all the causal issues that have occurred throughout the film is often done through the use of a high point of action, known as the climax. A personal favourite is Hitchcock's *North By Northwest* (1959) in which the climax shows the two main protagonists hanging off Mount Rushmore. Their pursuers have been killed, but can they save themselves? We have the two specific possible outcomes: either they will fall or they will survive.[14] Hitchcock resolves this outcome *and* ties up all the outstanding causal issues in less than 30 seconds and the film is over.

However, this type of ending – in which the climax is the end – is rare. For the majority of classical Hollywood narrative films there is a denouement after the climax; at least one final scene in which outstanding plot points or emotional aspects in relation to the protagonist/s

NOTES:

11 As always there are discrepancies, for example *Leaving Las Vegas* (1995), where the aim *is* the downfall.

12 Though some do come perilously close, such as *The Birds* (1963).

13 As opposed to 'open', when a film does not give a definitive conclusion. An example of this is Truffaut's *Les Quatre Cent Coups* (1959), where the film freezes on Antoine's face and so we do not learn whether he has permanently escaped from the reformatory or will be captured and sent back.

14 There is actually three: only one of them could fall – but this is a Hollywood film, so there is not a remote possibility of *that* happening.

1. Narrative (and Genre)

are resolved for the audience, if not the characters themselves. Back to *Psycho*. The climax of the film reveals that Norman Bates is the killer and we learn the 'truth' about his mother. He is also captured, closing down the causal chain of events. However, this climax cannot be the resolution of the film, because there are still two outstanding plot points in respect to the film's narrative: will Marion's body (and therefore the fate of the money) be found and why did Norman become a killer? As a result, Hitchcock has to include three final scenes in order to resolve these matters, so that both the audience and the characters within the film gain 'closure'.[15]

Furthermore, more recently, classical Hollywood narrative films have increasingly had more than one 'climax'. These 'double climaxes' (triple versions have been done, but on the whole these have not been successful in terms of audience response) invariably fall into two categories: the resurrected antagonist (any number of horror/hybrid horror films, but arguably *Alien* (1979) is still the best) and the unexpected second twist, either in terms of spectacle (*Poltergeist* (1982) is an excellent example of this) or, far more rarely, in terms of plot (*The Spanish Prisoner* (1997) and *The Salton Sea* (2001) being two examples).[16]

There is one last aspect of importance in terms of resolution in respect to classical Hollywood narrative, and that concerns the **emotional engagement** of the audience. Hollywood films may stimulate the head intellectually (fans have been baking their noodles over the meanings and symbolism in *The Matrix* (1999) ever since it was released, for example), but the heart is their primary aim. The resolution must be emotionally effective and the spectator emotionally affected. If the end of the film is emotionally satisfying, to a certain extent it does not matter if that end is comic or tragic, whether the emotion felt is one of happiness or sadness or a mixture of both (though Hollywood tends to prefer 'happy' endings, as commercially it believes they are more successful). It is not necessary to have the

audience leave the cinema feeling good to have a successful film, as long as they feel something – other than boredom or disappointment, that is. Mel Gibson alone has proved this twice with *Braveheart* (1995) and *The Passion of the Christ* (2004). However, to do this the resolution of a film must be both believable and consistent with what has gone before. This does not mean the film's ending has to be realistic in terms of reality itself, but in terms of the reality the film has created (film theorists refer to this as **verisimilitude**). If the film is set in outer space or under water, is about ghosts or talking mammals from the ice age, the audience long ago suspended their disbelief or else became disengaged, in which case the film has already failed. As such, as long as (1) the ending contains an emotional impact that is believable and consistent with the action that has come before it in terms of cause and effect and (2) the protagonists act consistently and believably, in that they stay true to the character traits and abilities they have previously exhibited, the film has achieved a successful resolution in terms of classical Hollywood narrative.

Lastly, classical Hollywood narrative relies on the storyteller and the audience understanding the same **formal conventions**. In other words, the film-makers and the audience know the same 'rules' or 'codes' that the film is operating within. These conventions, which vary in respect to the type of film being produced, will be explored in more detail in section two, but they are important in terms of narrative in that they provide a shared framework of reference between film-makers and audiences. The film-maker exploits these conventions in order to communicate certain aspects of the narrative quickly and effectively to the audience. For example, if a film opens on a character wearing a white Stetson, has a Colt-45 strapped to his waist and a metal star pinned to his jacket, the audience can reasonably assume that: (a) this film is a western, (b) the character they are looking at is a sheriff and (c) it is likely that he is the hero, as villains tend to dress in black (but see below). As a result of this, just as audience expectations

NOTES:

15 The psychologist's explanation of Norman's behaviour is the first; Norman's mother dominating Norman's thoughts is the second; Marion's car being dragged from the swamp as the final credits roll is the third.

16 Both these films have been mentioned because they actually contain three twists in the resolution, but their failures to light up the box office shows that audiences are not ready - or at least not yet willing - to deal with more than two.

can be directed in terms of narrative development, so certain audience expectations can be raised in terms of genre conventions, which can then be manipulated by the film-maker. In terms of classical Hollywood narrative, this manipulation takes the form of fulfilling these expectations by delivering what is expected (the conventional) and surprising the audience by delivering something unexpected (the original). Too much originality and the audience may become confused; too much conventionality and the audience may be disappointed. To return to our white-Stetsoned sheriff, if after seeing him, he then proceeds to shoot an unarmed man in the back, our expectations have immediately been undermined by the film-maker in that the 'rules' have been broken. In other words, the film-maker has manipulated the formal conventions of the western (good guys wear white; sheriffs do not shoot unarmed men; only the vilest of villains shoots someone from behind).

However, there is another set of conventions in classical Hollywood narrative that can also be used in order to deliver the conventional and the unexpected. These conventions are not to do with genre, but with editing, specifically **continuity editing**. This type of editing – the most common form used in Hollywood films and indeed world cinema – has at its basis the idea of linking shots together to tell the story of a film in such a way that the audience is not consciously aware of these cuts, which is why it is sometimes referred to as 'invisible editing'. The film-maker is not only concerned with this, however. An equally important concern, if not more important, is the process of joining these different shots in order to control how the story is presented in terms of what the audience sees and when they see it while retaining narrative coherence. As such, if a film's story is constructed along the principles of classical Hollywood narrative, certain approaches have to be undertaken.

The first of these is to ensure the story moves from its exposition to its resolution without irrelevant details. Continuity editing is thus used by the film-maker to control what events of the story are seen and what is not. A simple example of this is a sequence of a film in which the protagonist climbs into a car and drives off, followed by a cut to the same protagonist parking the same car in a different location. This is not considered to be an infringement of realism by the audience, rather a removal of unnecessary information. We do not need to see the drive from one location to the next, as we assume it is not important in terms of the film's narrative. We accept that classical Hollywood narrative only shows relevant information and does not show the irrelevant; we understand we do not need to see the protagonists' every movement. As such, we are cognisant that the unfolding of time in a film is both 'real' while it actually disregards certain aspects of it. This removal of unnecessary information is known as **elliptical editing**, as the events that occur take up less time on screen than they do in the story.

Secondly, the film-maker has to ensure the events occurring in the story are linked together, rather then arbitrary sequences that do not seem to relate to each other. This does not mean that other forms of editing such as rapid cutting, linkage editing or dialectical editing do not allow the audience to make connections, but rather that continuity editing makes these connections in a particular way, invariably by showing one event after another in a particular order to create a link between those events – sometimes referred to as the 'framing' of adjacent sequences. In other words, we are aware that a latter sequence occurs after the former in terms of time unless we have been 'informed' visually and/or verbally through a dissolve, a voice-over or through text that the film has moved backwards or forwards temporally, often by a date or year being shown. Both text (whether overlaid on visuals or through a title card) and the dissolve break the idea of continuity editing, but do so in the closest minimal way this type of editing has so far come up with.

Thirdly, the film has to make sense in terms of

NOTES:

1. Narrative (and Genre)

the audience being able to understand the events that are occurring in a clear, coherent way. Continuity editing ensures that the audience knows where and when the events are happening in relation to each other.

To assist in this process, certain editorial conventions have evolved over time. These include the establishing shot/close-up/re-establishing shot, the shot/reverse shot (this is almost always used either to show protagonists' actions/reactions or dialogue/response), the 180° rule, the 30° rule, constancy of direction, the eye-line match, point-of-view cutting, cross-cutting (a.k.a. parallel editing), match on action, the fade-in, the fade-out and the dissolve (a wipe can also be used, but in doing so the audience becomes consciously aware of an editing technique, and thus it cannot strictly speaking be considered a tool of continuity editing). Space forbids the exploration of all of these conventions, but any good general introduction to film studies should include an explanation of these techniques.

Narrative in *The Sixth Sense*

Having explored classical Hollywood narrative in general terms, it would seem that **The Sixth Sense** follows, with only the previously mentioned minor flashbacks, this narrative mode of storytelling. After all, it is clearly told through omniscient narrative, is character-driven through the two main protagonists, has a three-act structure that distinctly displays exposition, development and resolution which is linear both in terms of space and time, displays certain narrative codes and conventions that the film-maker shares with the audience and, judging by the enormous box-office receipts, was emotionally satisfying in respect to audience engagement.

In fact, not only does it appear to follow one particular narrative approach, it also seems to follow one particular type of narrative theory, namely that of Tzvetan Todorov's.

Todorov simplified the idea of narrative theory while also allowing a more complex interpretation of film texts with his theory of Equilibrium and Disequilibrium. The theory is as follows:

1 The fictional environment begins with a state of equilibrium (everything is as it should be).

2 It then suffers some form of disruption (disequilibrium).

3 New equilibrium is produced at the end of the narrative.

According to Todorov, in order to arrive at this new equilibrium, the narrative progresses through five stages:

1 A state of equilibrium.

2 A disruption of that order by an event.

3 A recognition that the disorder has occurred.

4 An attempt to repair the damage of the disruption.

5 A return to or restoration of a new equilibrium.

With Todorov's approach, although the narrative can be told in a linear fashion, the structure of the narrative itself is not linear but circular – as the narrative is driven by the protagonist/s' attempts to restore the equilibrium. However, the equilibrium attained at the end of the narrative is never identical to the equilibrium that was presented at the beginning. The narrative always involves a *transformation* of some kind. The characters or their situations are transformed through the progress of the disruption and this disruption usually takes place outside the 'normal' social framework or social events (in other words, the disruption is extraordinary in some way).

When Todorov's narrative theory is applied to **The Sixth Sense**, a clear relationship can be discerned. The initial equilibrium is that of Dr Malcolm Crowe (Bruce Willis) celebrating a successful and worthwhile career as a child psychologist, emphasised at the beginning of the

NOTES:

NARRATIVE (AND GENRE) | *The Sixth Sense*

film with the citation he has just received from the city of Philadelphia. Rather than showing Malcolm receiving this award as the opening sequence of the film, Shyamalan chooses instead to show him and his wife, Anna (Olivia Williams), at home after the ceremony. This is done so that, in terms of narrative brevity, the audience can be made immediately aware not only of Malcolm's success in terms of his chosen profession, but also that he has a successful and loving marriage. In this way, the initial equilibrium – through Malcolm's drunken Dr Seuss-like repartee with Anna – is seen as one of harmony and happiness both between husband and wife and between work and play.[17]

The disruption of this equilibrium in *The Sixth Sense* immediately follows this introduction. Vincent Gray (Donnie Wahlberg), a former patient who is angry with Malcolm for failing to help him, shoots Crowe and then kills himself.

Fig. 2: "You failed me!"

There follows a time-lapse in the narrative (specified as 'the next Fall' through text that also tells us we are still in Philadelphia), and Malcolm is next seen taking up the case of nine-year-old Cole Sear (Haley Joel Osment), a troubled child living with his mother Lynn (Toni Collette). At this point, the recognition of the disorder by Crowe is inferred by the audience rather than specifically stated, and is two-fold in nature. The first is that Malcolm has not been practising as a child psychologist for a period of time. The audience can infer this overtly as being due to the need for him to recover from his wounds, but a covert inference can also be made, namely that Crowe has lost confidence in himself in a professional capacity as a result of his failure to

help Vincent. The second recognition of disorder is in respect to Crowe's marriage and again is inferred by the audience rather than stated. Malcolm turns up late at the restaurant where he proposed to Anna and his wife walks out on him. From this, the audience is meant to conclude that the previously happy marriage is now strained.

What follows is Crowe's attempts to restore the equilibrium both in terms of his work and his marriage. He hopes to reclaim the belief he had in himself by succeeding in helping Cole's psychological wellbeing, as Cole's case is very similar to that of Vincent's – and in so doing, will once again become the man his wife loved and so regain the relationship they had.

To an extent, Malcolm succeeds in his aim. By the end of the film, Cole is a happier child who has begun to build a better relationship with his mother and is now accepted by his peers – and Malcolm learns that his wife still loves him while at the same time understands why she has distanced herself. A new equilibrium has been arrived at.

However, this seemingly apparent conventional following of a narrative approach in fact is a total subversion of it. By having Crowe appear in the majority of scenes of the film, Shyamalan is inviting the spectator to see the events that occur through Crowe's point of view. However, this point of view is revealed at the end of the film to be completely unreliable. The omniscient narrative we have been following is flawed, because both Malcolm and the audience are missing a vital piece of information. Malcolm does not know he is dead. Therefore, Shyamalan's narrative, particularly the shock ending, works specifically through a deliberate undermining of Todorov's narrative theory – in that the narrative is based on an incorrect (or rather incomplete) recognition of the disorder that has occurred in Malcolm's state of equilibrium. It is only when Malcolm acknowledges his death that his point of view becomes reliable and the spectator becomes cognisant that seemingly straightforward events in

NOTES:

17 Though there are hints this is not quite the case, they are deliberately underplayed.

1. Narrative (and Genre)

the film were actually loaded with ambiguity. Due to Malcolm's failure to recognise the nature of the disruption, his interaction with the other characters has been a fallacy. Conversations and events we thought we saw Crowe participating in we realise did not occur. Only Cole, a child who can see ghosts, sees him – and he does not directly inform us of such.

In essence, the narrative structure of *The Sixth Sense* is built around the idea of a *paradigm shift*, in that the film's dramatic climax results in the audience reconsidering everything they have seen previous to this in a new light. The information they receive at the end of the film causes them to re-evaluate many of the narrative events in an entirely different way. Our interpretation of these events has been radically altered due to a sudden and dramatic change in the narrative perspective.

Shyamalan has therefore constructed a narrative that can be read in two ways. The primary reading is one that supports the 'false' narrative; however, this primary reading contains information that allows a secondary reading to later occur. Sometimes, these clues are visual: the use of the colour red or drop in temperature when dead people are present, for example. At other times, the behaviour of the characters provides the clues: Cole running to the sanctuary of the church on first seeing Crowe, which Malcolm misinterprets as resistance to him as a new therapist (when in fact it is because he is a ghost). These clues can be retrospectively seen to be occurring from very early on in the film, an example being in the opening sequence; in fact the very first minute of the film. We see Malcolm's wife feeling suddenly colder in the cellar while looking for a celebratory bottle of wine.[18] The primary reading is that she belatedly realises how cold it is, understandable given the inference that she is already in a state of intoxication, which slows down our reaction to new stimuli. However, a retrospective secondary reading is that she has a little of the 'gift' Cole has, and feels the presence of spirits who have entered the house with Vincent, who is hiding upstairs in the bathroom[19] (supported by her

later discussion with potential buyers of a ring in her shop of her belief that previous owners of important objects leave a 'trace' of themselves within that object, and confirmed by her awareness of Malcolm's presence whilst dreaming during the climatic sequence).

Fig. 3: Anna in the cellar

Shyamalan does not merely manipulate conventional narrative expectations in terms of a character's unreliable point of view, however. He also uses the spectator's understanding of the formal conventions of continuity editing in order to undermine the narrative. Specifically he does this through both the framing of adjacent sequences and the point-of-view cuts within each sequence. An example of this is two sequences which appear back to back early in the film: the first being when we see Malcolm and Lynn waiting for Cole to return from school (entitled 'Mind Reading Games' on the British DVD release), followed by Cole seemingly talking to his wife in the restaurant where he proposed ('Anniversary Dinner').

In the former sequence, it seems Malcolm and Lynn are both aware of the other's presence due to their facing each other in chairs while they wait for Cole, shown through a wide shot – but on closer viewing, it can be seen that while Malcolm is looking at Lynn, she is not looking at Malcolm. This is reinforced by the fact that there is no shot/reverse shot between them, which is conventionally used to show character interaction in continuity editing, and further reinforced by the two-shots of Cole and Lynn together, while Malcolm is always shown alone throughout this sequence. When Cole returns, Lynn greets her son and talks quietly to him, including the

---

NOTES:

18 The preceding shot of her face being enclosed (by the wine-rack), emphasised by a camera push-in, is often used as a signifier of threat or danger. It is followed by a shot that stresses her shadow on the wall.

19 Shyamalan shot a version of this sequence where her breath becomes cold, but decided not to use it, as he felt this signifier that ghosts are present was being presented to the audience too soon.

(mis)telling lines 'You know, you can tell me things if you need to' and 'You got an hour', which the audience initially relates to Crowe's presence as a child psychologist. Combined with the inter-cuts of Crowe listening and reacting to this exchange (though significantly not looking at it), followed by his interaction with Cole through the mind-reading game while Lynn goes off to make triangle pancakes, this sequence leads us to believe all three have interacted, despite the fact they have not. That Malcolm does not say goodbye to Lynn after this unsuccessful session with Cole is assumed by the audience to be unimportant, again due to our understanding of continuity editing. We accept that we do not see this exchange as we believe it has no relevance to the story being told – except in **The Sixth Sense**, what we assume in terms of narrative convention is exactly what is played upon.

However, even if the spectator did begin to consider Crowe's non-verbal interaction with Lynn at the beginning of the sequence, Shyamalan ensures they do not get the chance, as he follows it with a sequence where Crowe goes into verbal overdrive. This scene, where Malcolm is 'late' for the anniversary of his proposal to Anna, has no verbal interaction between the two because Malcolm appears to dominate the (non-existent) conversation due to his desire to explain to his wife why he is late.[20] In doing so, he is covertly trying to inform her that he is attempting to again become the man he once was through his case with Cole. Anna seems to respond, as she looks at him (in actuality there is only one direct look and it is momentary; the rest are suggested, as the audience sees her physical 'responses' to Malcolm from behind rather than seeing her face – specifically small movements of her head),[21] but this recognition is entirely non-verbal until she says 'Happy anniversary'. On first viewing, this appears to be directed at Malcolm; it is only on subsequent viewing that the audience realises she is remembering their anniversary alone rather than together and this comment is actually a sad vocalisation to herself. However, unlike the previous sequence of cutting between Crowe,

Cole and Lynn, this time Shyamalan uses an entirely different stylistic and cinematographic approach. In the 'Mind Reading Games' sequence, there are 50 cuts; in the 'Anniversary Dinner' there are none. It is one continuous take using zoom, pull back and camera movement.

Fig. 4: The anniversary dinner

The 'Anniversary Dinner' sequence is not just filmed the way it is to make Anna's reactions ambiguous, but also to deliberately subvert narrative conventions in terms of the two sequences seen one after another. In doing this, Shyamalan not only uses the slow pace/fast pace approach that appears in many horror films – both classic and contemporary – but also deliberately places two key sequences together so that the audience only reads the apparent narrative concerns, rather than the hidden ones. What appears to be irony on Anna's part, after Malcolm talks of a case that is his second chance, is actually a private sadness. This is why Anna is wearing a red dress and why the table is only set for one. Malcolm does not even move the chair he sits on in the restaurant because he cannot affect physical objects (albeit this is seemingly later contradicted by his breaking of the glass of Anna's shop).

The analysis of the two sequences above is just one example of how Shyamalan deliberately subverts the conventions of classical Hollywood narrative not just in terms of content (characters, settings, etc.) but also through the treatment of continuity editing. He is aware that the spectator is knowledgeable of these conventions and accepts them, and thus uses our awareness of these conventions in order to 'hide' the unexpected twist. Equally, he uses this same

NOTES:

20 While also hinting to the audience of his actual physical state with the line 'I just can't seem to keep track of time'.

21 Ironically (and deliberately), the opening line of the sequence following this has Cole saying 'Stop looking at me' to Crowe while neither is clearly in shot.

1. Narrative (and Genre)

awareness to create subsequent spectator pleasure. Through repeated viewings, we become aware of how our understanding of classical Hollywood narrative has been manipulated through Shyamalan's subversion of formal conventions to both reveal and conceal the film's secret. In fact, this subsequent reading of the 'duality' of the narrative not only leads us to realise that the effectiveness of *The Sixth Sense* is based just as much on the manipulation of these formal narrative conventions as it is on the story itself, but that the subversion of these narrative conventions to tell a story is equally important in terms of connecting the audience and the protagonists.[22] Just as Crowe is not able to see the truth of his own death, despite all the evidence presented to him, so the audience is also not able to see the truth. The audience has also 'died' in terms of narrative realisation. *The Sixth Sense* not only subverts some of the formal conventions, it subverts almost all of them. By deliberately avoiding the use of shot/reverse shots, Shyamalan also avoids cuts of action/reaction and dialogue/response; his establishment/close-up/re-establishment shots, while ensuring narrative continuity, also mislead the audience in respect to Crowe's actual physical presence; and his framing of adjacent sequences that contain important information on several occasions – rather than the usual conventional approach of placing major next to minor until the resolution – means the audience do not have the chance to pick up all the clues as to what is actually occurring.

Finally, while *The Sixth Sense* does not break the 'closed ending' rule of classical Hollywood narrative, the audience does not get 'closure' in the usual sense, as the film plays with the audience's expectations of how a Hollywood film should end. Though we do not leave the cinema speculating as to what happens next, we do leave with questions of what happened *during*: what hints did we miss, what seemingly insignificant details actually were significant.

As such, Shyamalan achieves an impressive feat. He makes the unbelievable believable through a clear, linear, character-driven storyline, but does so by playing an elaborate narrative game with the audience, culminating in a surprise ending that forces the audience to entirely re-evaluate what they have been watching. At the end of *The Sixth Sense*, having suspended our disbelief, we realise that what we believed should not have been believed. In other words, Shyamalan makes the unbelievable believable and then unbelievable again.

The last half-decade of the twentieth century saw independent cinema breaking into the major commercial arena and an increasing number of films being produced that explored unconventional narrative structures. Along with the previously mentioned *Pulp Fiction* and *The Usual Suspects*, there was *Lost Highway* (1997), *Run Lola Run* (1998) and *Following* (1998). That half-decade ended with a bumper year for films undermining conventional narrative approaches. *Fight Club* (1999) created a secondary narrative reading via a character who did not exist; *American Beauty* (1999) had a resolution that did not actually resolve anything in terms of either the themes or the characters; *The Matrix* (1999) opened with a false equilibrium. And with *The Sixth Sense*, a mainstream, seemingly traditional and (some would say) old-fashioned film, another realm of narrative possibility was explored.

Hooray for Hollywood.

NOTES:

22 Though this may not be a conscious recognition in respect to the majority of the audience. (Why should it be? Most viewers go to enjoy a film, not analyse it.)

Genre: An Overview

An enormous number of texts have appeared in respect to film genre. Part of the reason for this is that film genres are constantly changing, so film theorists have to constantly revise their understanding of it. By its very nature, genre cannot be categorised, classified or generally 'nailed down' because of its constant evolution, both in terms of visual/aural minutiae and in terms of thematic and narrative developments. Some films add to a genre's **iconography** (visual conventions) in a small way, which is picked up by subsequent film-makers; others create an entirely new aspect or subversion which is then developed (or more often repeated) by film-makers who make a film in the same genre. The original, silent version of *The Cat and the Canary* (1927) is an example of the former. Its shots of long corridors with billowing curtains in a horror film have been repeatedly used in subsequent films in the horror genre. A more recent example of the latter is *The Last Seduction* (1994); not only does the *femme fatale* get away with the crime, but she is by far the strongest protagonist in a genre invariably reserved for strong men (if film noir can even be considered as a genre, which is still a subject of debate; the argument being that it was not acknowledged as such by either the film-makers or the audience at the time nor, it is contended, does it have specific stylistic or narrative approaches).[23]

However, despite all this, film genre is something that can be easily recognised. Ask a child what kind of film Dracula or Frankenstein appear in after they have watched an example of it and they can tell you it is a horror film, even if they were not scared by it. Similarly, these same children understand the idea of **hybrid genres** (a combination of two or more genres) even though they do not express it as such. *Alien* is understood by them to be both a horror and a science-fiction film (yes, your children have probably seen it even if you do not think they have), *Back to the Future Part III* (1990) a science-fiction film and a western, and *Blazing Saddles* (1974) a western and a comedy. *Outland* (1981) is not only a western set in space, it is one particular western (*High Noon*). In fact, when analysed closely, it can be argued that *Star Wars* (1977) contains more codes and conventions belonging to the western than those associated with science-fiction.

So, what is genre? Essentially, genre is an ever-growing body of films that share the same visual and narrative codes and conventions. In terms of the audience, this helps them to select what film they would like to see at the cinema or pay-per-view channels, or choose to watch on satellite or terrestrial television, because different spectators like different types of film. Your average teenager is unlikely to want to watch Tarkovsky's *Andrei Rublyov* (1969) for example, just as women on the whole are unlikely to be interested in seeing Russ Meyer's *Beneath the Valley of the Ultra-vixens* (1979). In terms of the film industry, genre is useful in terms of making, promoting and selling films in two ways. Firstly, the success (and failure) of certain genre films allows the industry to 'track' what types of film audiences want and so what types to make. Though Maltby has argued that Hollywood production is concerned more with **cycles** of films than with genres,[24] where the aim is to imitate previous films that have recently been successful (the obvious example being sequels, which are considered 'pre-sold' by the industry, as the audience who saw the original film return to the sequel in order to repeat the experience), these cycles show that certain film genres grow and fade in popularity. For example, the musical has risen to the fore several times in the history of cinema and enjoyed another recent (minor) renaissance through the successes of *Moulin Rouge!* (2001), *Hedwig and the Angry Inch* (2001), *Chicago* (2002), *8 Mile* (2002) – which is a musical, albeit of a different sort – and

NOTES:

23 It can also be argued whether *The Last Seduction* was a major addition to/subversion of the film noir 'genre'. To begin with, is it film noir or neo-noir? (Can any noir film in colour be considered film noir? If not, how do you classify *Chinatown* (1974) or *The Big Fix* (1978), two films that are clearly built on film noir genre conventions and themes of the 1940s and 1950s - and does that mean that *The Two Jakes* (1990), *Chinatown*'s sequel, is a neo-neo-noir!?). Secondly, is *The Last Seduction* merely a development on the genre subversion of *Basic Instinct* (1992); and was this anything more than a development from *Body Heat* (1981) … and so on.

24 Maltby, *Hollywood Cinema*, 2003.

2. Genre (and Themes)

Camp (2003), before being firmly halted by the failure of the Cole Porter-goes-Pop *De-Lovely* (2004). Even more recently we have seen the resurrection of the biopic with *The Aviator* (2004), *Beyond the Sea* (2004), *Ray* (2004), *The Life and Death of Peter Sellers* (2004), *Kinsey* (2004) and *Walk the Line* (2005). Under Maltby's argument, these films came about because of the critical and commercial successes of *A Beautiful Mind* (2001), *Iris* (2001) and *Monster* (2003) and they may well have done so in Hollywood industry thinking, but each biopic is very different from the other by their very nature (the story of a female serial killer and a sexologist do not have a lot in common). Audiences did not suddenly become desirous of biographical films; they responded to each one on an individual basis. Time will tell whether the others succeed or not, but their success or failure will depend on how good they are as films, not because they belong to a particular cycle. However, even if the idea of cycles is accepted, these cycles can vary. The biblical and Roman epics of the early 1950s – made partly to exploit the new technological development of widescreen format – have now reappeared in the form of Greek and Roman epics such as *Gladiator* (2000), *Troy* (2004) and *Alexander* (2004).

Secondly, genre allows the industry to pre-sell and package films to audiences through a shared understanding of generic codes. Advertising and promotional imagery (ranging from press packs to merchandise) use these codes to 'sell' the film to audiences. When was the last time you saw a poster for a western that did not include a cowboy hat, riding coat and a rifle and/or six-gun?

More than this, though, genre allows audiences to both have their expectations fulfilled and experience something new. Essentially, genre films walk a fine line between aspects that are predictable and expected – the formulaic – and delivering aspects that are surprising and interesting – the unexpected. An effective genre film has to balance these two requirements: too much of the former and the audience is disappointed because there was nothing new; too much of the latter and the audience is disappointed because their expectations were not fulfilled. Or, as Goldman (again) wrote, 'give the audience what they want, but not in the way that they expect it.' [25]

However, generic classifications are not enough. To go back to the example of the teenager and Tarkovsky, while he or she may not wish to view *Andrei Rublyov*, how about Tarkovsky's *Solyaris* (1972) or *Stalker* (1979)? Both these films (the former especially) could be classified as belonging to the science-fiction genre, yet neither is likely to be appreciated or even be considered a 'real' sci-fi film by a teenage spectator. This is where sub-genres come in.

Sub-genres again allow both the industry and the audience to target and choose what films they think they would like to experience. To turn to the comedy genre, different audiences like different types of comedy. Someone who likes slapstick/screwball comedy may not like satire and visa versa. As such, there are sub-genres of comedy: parody, romantic comedy, farce, black comedy, etc. Crime genre is an even better case in point. The murder mystery is very different to the caper, which is different to the thriller, detective, legal/courtroom, espionage or prison drama sub-genres and indeed film noir, which may be based in terms of story on any of the above, but will include elements that are distinct from any of them. Even the mocumentary (fiction presented as documentary) which, it can be argued, is the newest genre type to have appeared and so contains fewer examples in its canon, has clear distinctions. *This is Spinal Tap* (1984) may be a mocumentary comedy like *Zelig* (1983), but they do not appeal to exactly the same audience. *Bob Roberts* (1992) seems to be targeted at a different one and *Man Bites Dog* (1992) definitely is. *A Mighty Wind* (2003) is a mocumentary directed and co-written by Christopher Guest, the same writer as *This is Spinal Tap*, but each is aimed at different audiences (or perhaps the same audience who has grown older between the films). [26]

NOTES:

25 Goldman, ibid, 1983.

26 *Best in Show* (2000) was also co-written and directed by Guest and seems to be primarily aimed at a very unusual crossover audience, namely dog lovers! It is a multi-generational approach at least.

There is also one other type of genre, though it is not recognised by all genre theorists. This is the **supra-genre**. McKee writes about it in the following way:

> …for those that believe that genres and their conventions are concerns of 'commercial' writers only, and that serious art is nongeneric… the avant-garde notion of writing outside the genres is naïve. No one writes in a vacuum. After thousands of years of storytelling no story is so different that it has no similarity to anything else ever written. The Art Film has become a traditional genre… [it] is a supra-genre that embraces other basic genres… [27]

Supra-genre is not the same as hybrid genre, because it is not simply the combination of two or more genres, but a particular way of presenting those genre combinations in terms of narrative and style. In respect to art films, this usually occurs through the absence of stars – often associated with particular genres – or at least star salaries; production methods and approaches outside the Hollywood system;[28] and a strong usage of at least one of the following: enigmatic characters, visual symbolism, inconclusive resolutions, non-linear narratives and unconventional stylistic approaches. It could also be argued that the historical drama, the biography (and its sub-genre, the autobiography), the docu-drama, the musical and animation genres are all actually supra-genres, but as I am not a recognised film theorist, I will let somebody else make the effort. The concept of supra-genre is worth considering, however.

A genre approach to film immediately hits a problem, though. Simply put, if certain visual and narrative codes and conventions define a film's genre placement, how can a film be considered an example of a particular genre *before* those visual and narrative codes and conventions had been developed? To put it another way, how can a horror film be classified as a horror film at a time when no codes and conventions for a horror film were in existence? Even if the film is classified as such retrospectively, how many codes and conventions should it contain? It is said that the Lumière Brothers ***Arrivée d'un Train en Gare á la Ciotat***, a.k.a ***The Arrival of a Train at La Ciotat*** (1895), sent people running out of the auditorium screaming in fear of being hit by the locomotive, thus it was certainly horrifying to them, but it can hardly be classified as a horror film. ***Das Kabinett des Doktor Caligari***, a.k.a. ***The Cabinet of Dr Caligari*** (1919), is considered by a number of theorists as one of the major sources of horror films, as well as being an important example of German Expressionism, and therefore could be argued as being the first 'true' horror film. However, if this is the case, where does it leaves films such as ***Der Golem*** (1915), ***Life Without Soul*** (1915) or indeed the four films based on Robert Louis Stevenson's *Dr Jekyll and Mr Hyde* released between 1908 and 1913?

Furthermore, to return to genre development and the use of codes and conventions, how much can a film subvert or ignore a particular genre's codes and conventions and still be classified as being in the same genre? If part of the nature of genre films should be the presentation of something original and unexpected, at what point does a genre theorist draw the line? If a film is set in the future, but contains no futuristic science or technology, no aliens or mutations, no stylistic conventions that occur in science-fiction films, can it be classified as a science-fiction film? The answer would seem to be 'no'. Starting a film with the words 'The Year is 2102' and then showing a world exactly like the one we currently inhabit is not a science-fiction film; it has to incorporate some kind of futuristic – or more specifically a scientific futuristic – reference. So, a film showing a world that resembles ours precisely and is a story about love and loss, for example, cannot be classified as a science-fiction film. How about if it shows a futuristic-looking building at the end, without any other codes and conventions associated with science-fiction? Surely that limited amount of mise-en-scène does not make it a science-fiction film. And if we are informed about only one piece of futuristic technology, also in the

---

NOTES:

27 McKee, *Story*, 1997.

28 Increasingly this is not the case, however. The purchasing of independent companies by the studios (such as Disney's acquisition of Miramax) or the studios themselves forming companies to develop less mainstream product, has resulted in a number of releases that could be classified as supra-genre art films being made by commercially aware but artistically idiosyncratic film-makers that would not otherwise have reached such a wide audience without studio backing and star involvement. Directors such as P.T. Anderson (*Magnolia*), Wes Anderson (*The Royal Tenenbaums* (2001)), David Fincher (*Fight Club*), Spike Jonze (*Adaptation* (2002)), Christopher Nolan (*Memento* (2000)), Alexander Payne (*Sideways* (2004)) and David O.Russell (*I Heart Huckabees* (2004)), along with the writer Charlie Kaufman, have become part of the Hollywood system in a way that has not been seen since the 'New Hollywood' era that existed between 1967and 1975.

denouement, does that *ipso facto* make it a science-fiction film? What is the minimum amount of narrative, thematic and stylistic codes and conventions needed before a film can be classified as belonging to the science-fiction genre?

If all the above sounds like mere sophistic positing – a theoretical film that does not exist – I have just described **Abre Los Ojos**, a.k.a. **Open Your Eyes** (1997), and its Hollywood remake **Vanilla Sky** (2001). For the majority of both films, there is almost nothing in the way of codes and conventions that marks either of them as a science-fiction film; and even when the audience does learn that these films are set in a 'virtual' environment (or mind in this case), there is little that follows the science-fiction genre. One piece of futuristic technology (the means to implant an alternative life in the brain of a cryogenically frozen body) should not a science-fiction film make, yet both films can be classified as a science-fiction hybrid without too much argument. As a contrast, **Eternal Sunshine of the Spotless Mind** (2004) also uses the idea of altering memories (this time by the removal of them) and does so with far more technological emphasis; moreover it uses special effects in a more obvious way, but it would be difficult to argue that it belongs in the science-fiction canon except in a very loose sense.

As Redmond comments in his analysis of **Blade Runner** (1982):

> If one were to examine, for example, the B-movie science fiction films of the 1950s with their 1990 counterparts one would, in the main, discover a world of difference in terms of imagery, special effects and narrative concerns. [29]

In other words, if the narrative is entirely different in construction than previous science-fiction films (**2001: A Space Odyssey** (1968) broke a whole bunch of narrative sci-fi conventions in one swift move); the imagery is a radical alteration (John Carpenter's **Dark Star** (1974) is an excellent example – the film world's

first 'dirty' spaceship?) or the special effects entirely different to previous films in the science-fiction genre (**Terminator 2** (1991) and its use of 'morphing'; **The Matrix** in terms of 'bullet time'), how can they be compared to science-fiction films such as **It Came From Outer Space** (1953), **Them** (1954), **Invasion of the Body Snatchers** (1956) or **Forbidden Planet** (1956), let alone **Plan Nine from Outer Space** (1959)! It is a real struggle to even make comparisons with 'high art' science-fiction films such as **Metropolis** (1927) or **Things to Come** (1936). The science-fiction films of the last two decades do not resemble those of the 1930s to 1950s, so how can we use codes and conventions to classify films in terms of genre when those very same codes and conventions can be broken so radically? No genre theorist would attempt to refute the claim that **2001, Dark Star, Terminator 2** or **The Matrix** are science-fiction films; yet at the time they were released they broke those same codes and/or conventions in major ways.

Further difficulties arise when one considers other factors that affect genre films. Over the last 30 years (though it actually began in the 1950s), there has been a notable 'juvenilisation' of cinema, in that the target audiences for films have become younger. For example, many horror films are now aimed more at a teenage audience than an adult one. This has meant that both the content and the treatment of the genre have changed in order to cater to this different audience. Though some of these horror films may seem graphic in terms of their visual content, this is due to the relaxing of film classification codes and changes in society's tastes and values. Audiences now are more accustomed to seeing sequences of graphic violence and explicit sex. However, even today, a horror film aimed at teenagers will not include a young girl masturbating with a crucifix as **The Exorcist** (1973) did. Furthermore, contemporary audiences are much more sophisticated in terms of genre expectations and recognition. While **Scream** (1998), a film that self-consciously parodies the genre conventions of the horror

NOTES:

29 Redmond, *Studying Blade Runner*, 2003.

movie, may contain similar conventions as *Halloween* (1978) and *Friday the Thirteenth* (1980) – not to mention the 25 'slasher' films that appeared in the 1981 top 50 box-office successes – can it truly be approached in terms of genre study in the same way as *The Exorcist* or *Dracula* (1931)?

Genre theory, then, is problematic but it does have it uses, which will now be applied to *The Sixth Sense*.

Genre in *The Sixth Sense*

The Sixth Sense is a hybrid genre film. Just exactly what type of hybrid genre it is – supernatural thriller, psychological horror or something else – will be examined shortly. That aside, it is a horror movie, a traditional horror movie even (the fear and suspense it creates can clearly be compared to the 'classic' horror films of yesteryear that created those feelings through suggestion and narrative development, rather than a dependency on visceral imagery that leaves nothing to the imagination and shocking moments with little or no build-up). However, the horror genre contains different 'types' of horror, so it is useful to consider which of these types *The Sixth Sense* belongs to.

Todorov, analysing horror in terms of literature, yet again developed an approach that can be applied to film. He determined the horror genre as having three distinctive forms: the 'uncanny', the 'marvellous' and the 'fantastic'.[30]

The **uncanny** is the 'supernatural explained'. This is any story (and thus film) in which seemingly irrational and inexplicable events actually have a rational explanation. As such, it includes not just a particular branch or sub-division of the horror genre (which is different from sub-genre, as it is one permutation of the horror genre rather than a specific type),[31] but also both the psychological thriller sub-genre and, to a lesser extent, the sci-fi/horror hybrid genre. The former usually contains a protagonist who is a victim of a 'conspiracy' to drive them mad by other human protagonists, invariably for financial gain or other worldly reasons (*Taste of Fear* (1961) is a classic example). The latter contains aliens or other creatures that are 'monstrous' in some way; they are a threat to humanity either by intention (*The Thing From Another World* (1951) and its 1982 remake *The Thing*) or unintentionally (*The Beast From 20,000 Fathoms* (1953)). It may seem that an enormous carnivorous dinosaur running rampage through New York City can hardly be considered rational, but the dinosaur – a rhedosaurus to be precise – is part of the natural order in terms of the film's verisimilitude. Its existence is rationally explained within the film (it is revived as a result of nuclear testing in the Arctic).

The **marvellous** is strange and incomprehensible events that can only be explained through accepting the existence of the 'supernatural'. As Strinati describes it, himself quoting from Todorov:

This reality differs radically from normal experience. Unlike the uncanny, the reader is lead to conclude that 'new laws of nature must be entertained to account for the phenomena'… This is what defines the marvellous, the acceptance of another level of reality to explain 'events… which are… incredible, extraordinary, shocking, singular, distributing or unexpected.'[32]

In other words, in films of this sub-division, the supernatural becomes visible in some way to the protagonists and/or the audience. Creatures such as the demon, the vampire and the zombie can only be accepted, not explained.[33] The events may occur through the protagonists' actions such as moving into a haunted house (*Thir13en Ghosts* (2001)) or through deliberate/accidental conjuring of the supernatural through invocation (*Rosemary's Baby* (1968) is an example of the former; *The Evil Dead* (1981) the latter). Alternatively, the supernatural comes to this world uninvited (*The Exorcist*). In *Poltergeist*, initially only the spectator is aware of the supernatural encroachment, as the child cannot express it as such (thus providing the classic tag-line of 'They're here'). In fact, under this sub-

NOTES:

30 Todorov, *The Fantastic: A structural approach to a literal concept*, 1973.

31 For example, the 'slasher' movie - a sub-genre of the horror film - could give uncanny or marvellous explanations of the events to the audience. In fact, the Halloween sequels have moved Michael Myers' character inexorably from the uncanny to the marvellous - with the exception of *Halloween III: The Season of the Witch* (1982), which ignored him altogether - while remaining within this sub-genre.

32 Strinati, *An Introduction to Studying Popular Culture*, 2000.

33 In fact, a scientific explanation is given in the first modern zombie film, *Night of the Living Dead* (1968): re-animation has occurred through radiation from a military satellite. However, it is suggested as a possibility rather than a certainty and occurs in the background instead of being highlighted. As such, the audience is not overtly made aware of the explanation. Rational explanations were certainly not given in many subsequent zombie movies.

2. Genre (and Themes)

division, neither the audience nor the protagonists need actually 'see' the supernatural in physical form, an example being ***The Entity*** (1981).

The **fantastic** (which McKee calls the 'super-uncanny')[34] is when no definite conclusion is given in respect to the causes of the inexplicable events that occur. In other words, in terms of film, the spectator is not given the closed ending traditionally delivered in classical Hollywood narrative. We are not explicitly informed whether these events occurred through rational causes (thus uncanny) or through supernatural intervention (thus marvellous). Therefore, the fantastic leads the spectator, as Todorov puts it, 'to hesitate between a natural and a supernatural explanation of the events described'.[35] This type of horror film is far less common than the first two types, but there are some notable examples. In ***Cat People*** (1942), a woman believes she is descended from a race of creatures that turn into murderous cats when kissed. However, it is never made explicit whether the events we see are the result of a supernatural occurrence or the hallucinations of her unbalanced mind. Similarly, in ***The Shining*** (1980) we leave the film uncertain as to whether the axe-wielding protagonist has gone insane or is genuinely possessed by malevolent spirits from the hotel's past.

However, if one decides to apply Todorov's structural approach, it is initially difficult to define what kind of horror film ***The Sixth Sense*** is. There are no motives of greed, lust or other secular reasons that lead to Cole experiencing what he does, and Crowe's motivations are positive ones (to help a child and redeem himself) and as such it is not uncanny. Similarly, it is clearly not fantastic, as the spectator is given an unmistakable and unambiguous supernatural explanation of the events seen by the end of the film. However, it is not obviously marvellous, because for the greater portion of the film, the audience does not know there is a supernatural element to it. Even when Cole informs Crowe that he sees 'dead people', we cannot be certain

this is so. Anything seen by the audience after this point could still be the product of a disturbed imagination of an unhappy child. It is only the last third of the film, more specifically during the funeral gathering for Kyra Collins (Mischa Barton) where Cole presents the evidence that the girl had been poisoned due to listening to her ghost, that the supernatural makes its presence felt beyond all doubt.

The reason for this is that ***The Sixth Sense*** does not start off as a horror film, but *becomes* one. By the end of the film, Todorov's definition of the marvellous in horror is the sub-division that should be applied. However, it still begs the question as to what type of film does ***The Sixth Sense*** appear to be for a significant portion of its duration?

The Sixth Sense has been described both as a 'psychological horror' and a 'supernatural thriller'. However, while it can be argued that the film is both psychological and a thriller, it is only so on a surface level. Yes, there is a mystery to solve: a mystery of the mind. What is the cause of Cole's anguish? Yet the resolution reveals that the real mystery – and the consequent thrill – is not one we are meant to be aware of throughout the film, nor is Cole's suffering due to psychological reasons. The thrilling part of ***The Sixth Sense*** is the spectator discovering Crowe is dead, not that Cole can see ghosts (this revelation is actually filmed in a low-key way, whereas a thriller would invariably heighten the explanation of the mystery). So, though ***The Sixth Sense*** can be classified as a horror/thriller hybrid genre film, the thriller aspect is somewhat downplayed.

The psychological part of ***The Sixth Sense*** is false for two reasons. Firstly, Cole does not have a mental difficulty, as the ghosts who haunt him are real in terms of the film's verisimilitude and once Cole accepts their visitations, the film makes it clear he is a happier child, both in terms of peer acceptance (the school play) and in terms of his relationship with his mother (convincing her he sees ghosts, thus explaining the strange

NOTES:

34 McKee, ibid, 1997.

35 Todorov, ibid, 1973.

occurrences she has witnessed around him that have worried her). Secondly, film theorists' definition of the psychological horror sub-genre only partly matches *The Sixth Sense*. It is a sub-genre that appeared mainly between the 1930s and 1950s and has at its basis the intention of emotionally engaging the audience through atmosphere and suspense (which *The Sixth Sense* does), that the horror presented is fantastic (as stated above, *The Sixth Sense* cannot be classified as such) and contains 'themes of alienation, paranoia and fantasy'[36] (while alienation can be considered a theme in *The Sixth Sense*, paranoia and fantasy are not). *The Sixth Sense*, then, while clearly being a hybrid genre, is strangely elusive when determining exactly what genres it is a hybrid of.

As such, perhaps *The Sixth Sense* can be approached from a very different genre perspective. Though it may seem absurd on first consideration, the film could be viewed as an example of an extremely unusual hybrid genre, the horror melodrama – more specifically, the supernatural melodrama.[37] While it is not usually described as such, or indeed appears to be so on initial viewing, if one looks at the prominent themes, they are very similar to those that appear in a genre often defined as a 'woman's genre'. This may explain part of the reason why this film was so successful, as it certainly appealed as much to women as men, a rare crossover in terms of the horror genre.[38] Even rarer, as Shyamalan comments on, was the discovery a few weeks into the theatrical release that the two main types of audience seeing the film were 'young boys and older women and they usually have nothing in common. They don't go to see the same movies; they don't care about the same things'.[39]

One of the purposes of the melodrama is to explore moral conflicts and dilemmas as experienced by ordinary people on a personal level. The reason why melodrama is often considered to be a woman's genre is that, as Buckland succinctly puts it:

… it represents the questions, problems, anxieties, difficulties and worries of women living in a male-dominated, or patriarchal, society. The first and most prevalent property, or common attribute, of melodrama is that it is dominated by an active female character.[40]

At this point, it would seem ridiculous to consider *The Sixth Sense* as a melodrama, because neither of the two main protagonists is female.[41] Yet if one looks at the common genre attributes of the melodrama, there are a number of correlations between it and *The Sixth Sense*. To begin with, melodrama – in terms of narration – often reflects a 'victim's' perspective, in that the major character is shown to be suffering in some way. Obviously, though Cole can be seen as a victim, he is not a victim in respect to a moral conflict. Similarly, though Crowe is also a victim, again it is not due to moral issues and the nearest he could be said to be suffering from a melodramatic conflict is that of trying to regain his wife's love when she seems to be developing a relationship with another man, as opposed to the other way around (which would have been more in line with the melodrama genre). However, as Crowe is eventually revealed to be dead, even this 'neo-melodrama' possibility is negated. Yet there is a female character who is suffering a moral dilemma and that is Lynn, Cole's mother. Fiercely protective of her son, she is shown in the film to be torn between her maternal love for her child, her bewilderment over what is happening to him and her fear that he is 'disturbed'. Throughout almost the entire film, she wavers between the belief that he is exhibiting this behaviour because he is being bullied and the possibility that this behaviour is self-engendered, as he appears to be a liar, a thief and possibly a self-harmer.[42] Though she is not a central character, she can be considered as the third main protagonist and her dilemma (mother-love versus parental concern) is certainly one of the major sub-themes of the film. In fact, more screen time

NOTES:

36 Jancovich, Horror, 1992.

37 I can think of only one other recent example, being *The Others* (2001).

38 Though not as rare as Hollywood analysts would have us believe. A lot of women may go to horror films because their male partners want to see them, but (if my female students and acquaintances are anything to go by) they want to watch them of their own accord, with or without male company.

39 *The Sixth Sense* 2 Disc Collector's Edition DVD, 2002.

40 Buckland, *Film Studies*, 1998.

41 Although it can be argued there is such a thing as 'male melodramas', the most prominent examples being the James Dean films *Rebel Without A Cause* (1955), *East of Eden* (1955) and *Giant* (1956).

42 While Lynn does not want to admit it in respect to the latter, this has been previously suggested by Crowe's diagnosis. Though Crowe rejects the possibility of self abuse, he does consider it - and the spectator is aware that his psychological conclusions have been fundamentally flawed on at least one occasion (though we are later informed that Crowe really could not have made a correct diagnosis in respect to Vincent from a rational point of view).

2. Genre (and Themes)

is devoted to this dilemma than Crowe's estrangement from his wife.[43]

Another main characteristic of the melodrama is that it uses an omniscient form of narration. *The Sixth Sense* is not merely dominated by the narrative perspective of two protagonists rather than one – thus immediately making it omniscient – it actually uses four: Cole's, Malcolm's, Lynn's and Anna's. This multiple approach to narration is a key element of the melodrama (see almost any Douglas Sirk film: *Magnificent Obsession* (1954) and *Written On The Wind* (1956) possibly being his two greatest examples).[44]

The melodrama invariably also narrates the story of more than one character; *The Sixth Sense* clearly tells the stories of two, Cole's and Malcolm's. Furthermore, these two stories are told both separately and through intertwining, again an approach often used in melodrama. Other important aspects that define a melodrama include unexpected twists of plot, the withholding of secrets and dramatic developments that create moral conflicts. *The Sixth Sense* contains two major plot twists and several minor ones; the withholding of a secret (Cole sees dead people) is a key element; moral conflicts occur through Lynn's love of her son and her fear that he is suffering from some kind of emotional and/or behavioural difficulty, Crowe's conflict between his seemingly collapsing relationship with his wife and his need to work with Cole (for both the boy's and his own sake), and Cole's desire to tell his mother about what is happening to him and his awareness that she will not believe him. It could even be argued (though stretching the point) that a chance event – another aspect of the melodrama – occurs in *The Sixth Sense* when Malcolm sees Anna's interaction with a potential lover while watching her through her shop window. He did not expect to see it and reacts violently when he does (this sequence certainly appears to be the only example in the film where Malcolm actually affects the physical world, though again his cracking of the window is inferred rather than seen directly).

Fig. 5: The cracked glass of the shop window

As such, *The Sixth Sense* contains a number of melodramatic aspects. The fact that a woman's point of view does not dominate the film in terms of narration or that the film does not focus on moral conflicts experienced by women within a patriarchal society does not *ipso facto* mean *The Sixth Sense* cannot be classified as a melodrama. *The Sixth Sense* was not created to reflect the thematic or stylistic approaches of one particular genre. Shyamalan deliberately attempted to write and direct a hybrid genre film. What is being considered here is that the hybrid genre combinations used are not the ones that seem apparent on initial viewing. Shyamalan – though perhaps not consciously (I suspect otherwise) – has made a film that is actually more than a supernatural thriller or a psychological horror. In effect, it can be argued that *The Sixth Sense* is a triple hybrid – a supernatural melodramatic mystery – once it undergoes close analysis.

The idea of *The Sixth Sense* being a supernatural melodrama will be further explored in section three. What can be concluded, though, is that while *The Sixth Sense* appears to be a 'traditional' type of horror film, in fact it is bringing a very contemporary genre approach to this tradition. Whether it is ultimately classified as a supernatural thriller, psychological horror or otherwise, both classic and contemporary genre approaches are present within the film, not only in terms of the horror genre itself but also in terms of playing with the idea of the hybrid genre. In *The Sixth Sense*, Shyamalan clearly shows his awareness of genre history and approach, and, equally clearly, delights in playing with both, without ever sacrificing audience pleasure. Not bad for a 28-year-old making his first major-league studio movie.

NOTES:

43 It does not seem this way because of the time spent at the beginning of the film showing Malcolm and Anna together rather than estranged.

44 *Written on the Wind* can also be considered a 'male melodrama', as its narrative is concerned with men as victims.

3. Themes and Characterisation

No matter how you consider *The Sixth Sense* – as an exceptionally clever, superbly crafted film full of suspense or an overworked, kitsch piece of fluff that takes itself far too seriously – there is no doubt its young director was not afraid to take on the big themes. Love, death, mortality, redemption: all these and more besides (alienation and isolation for example) are reflected on to a greater or lesser extent within the film.

However, the main theme explored in *The Sixth Sense* is that of **communication**. As Shyamalan himself commented, 'Everyone learning to communicate is kind of the point of the movie.'[45] The need to communicate, and the fears that stop people from doing so, appears in several guises in this film and, indeed, envelops all the other themes. It is predominantly considered metaphorically through Cole and the ghosts that haunt him, but it is also explored in a more literal way through the various dynamics between the characters. The primary dynamic in *The Sixth Sense* is the relationship between Malcolm and Cole, but as that relationship develops and eventually reaches an outcome, it directly affects the two secondary dynamics: Malcolm's and Anna's failing marriage and Cole and Lynn's collapsing family ties. A tertiary dynamic is also to do with communication. Malcolm's belief that he 'failed' Vincent, and his desire for absolution as a result of this failure, discretely drives the primary dynamic forward (or at least is its causal factor) and, ironically, it is his close listening to a recorded session with Vincent while he was literally not communicating – he had left the room – that leads Malcolm to both realising Cole is telling the truth and arriving at a solution to Cole's situation. Vincent, then, is a symbol for failed communication. His suicide after shooting Crowe in the opening sequence sets up the film's major theme: if we do not break through our barriers, do not trust others and communicate with them, we will destroy ourselves.

Therefore, communication, or rather the lack of it, between Cole and Crowe, between Malcolm

and his wife Anna, between Cole and his mother Lynn, dominates *The Sixth Sense*. And it is how these characters, specifically the two main protagonists, overcome their fears and take the step to 'only connect' (as E.M. Forster stressed at the beginning of *Howard's End*) that drives the narrative forward and brings about its resolution.

To begin with, the main plot point that ostensibly drives the narrative forward is Cole's 'secret'. It is not until 48 minutes and 25 seconds into the film that Malcolm is told that secret and it is only done so after Crowe himself opens up to Cole through a 'bedtime story' that actually tells how his own life has fallen apart:

> Once upon a time there was this person named Malcolm. He worked with children. He loved it… And then one night, he found out that he made a mistake with one of them. He couldn't help that one. And he can't stop thinking about it. He can't forget. Ever since then, things have been different. He's not the same person that he used to be. And his wife doesn't like the person that he's become. They barely speak anymore. They're like strangers. And then one day, Malcolm meets this wonderful little boy… Reminds him a lot of the other one. And Malcolm decides to try and help this new boy 'cause he feels that if he can help this new boy, it will be like helping that other one too.

As a result of this honesty, Cole reciprocates by telling Malcolm his secret of seeing dead people, and in doing so tacitly asks Crowe for his help. As such both protagonists, having finally vocalised their fears, begin the journey to overcome them that takes up the rest of the film. This is partly why the first section of *The Sixth Sense* is so slow compared to contemporary Hollywood output; why Shyamalan, as Gilbey puts it, 'slows the action to the speed of a funeral procession – a funeral procession in rush hour'.[46] Both story and character development have to be built slowly not just in order to hide the film's twist, but also to ensure that the film's major theme resonates with the audience. Cole's

---

NOTES:

45 *The Sixth Sense* 2 Disc Collector's Edition DVD, 2002.

46 Gilbey, *It Don't Worry Me*, 2003.

3. Themes and Characterisation

decision to finally reveal his secret to Malcolm is the dramatic lynchpin in terms of the plot, but it has to be done in a low-key way in order not to undermine the power of the narrative's real surprise – that Crowe is dead.

The reality is **The Sixth Sense** could have ended on an emotional high of Cole finally telling his mother what he sees. Convincing Lynn he sees ghosts through his explanation that his grandmother has been wanting to tell her she secretly saw her on stage could have been a satisfactory resolution of the film. Cole is happier, his mother now understands what has been troubling him and Crowe has exorcised his demons – and it is meant to lead the audience to the false conclusion that the film has reached its resolution. The 'journey' all the characters have been on has been witnessed and satisfactorily concluded. All that is left is the film's last remaining sub-plot, which we assume will also be resolved. Malcolm will tell Anna what he has experienced and we expect their relationship will be rebuilt through the inference that once she has listened to it she will understand. We do not need to see it; we just have to be informed it has begun. This would not have made a bad film and (though we will never know) probably not an unsuccessful one. But this film's final twist is built on what we expect in a denouement: that any remaining sub-plots will be resolved after the climax. We need to know the protagonists have got off Mount Rushmore. The fact that **The Sixth Sense** does not do this, delivers not just an unexpected final twist, but an incredibly powerful one, is precisely why (beyond all expectations) it was such a massive box-office hit.

Though he did not know that at the time, Shyamalan did know the key to this film's success: that the audience *cares* about the characters. In order to do this, he has to make sure the audience relates to, and is involved in, the anguish the two main protagonists feel. Just as Cole and Crowe connect with each other, so we must connect with them. This cannot be done just through words, but through actions and reactions, looks and glances – in a word,

nuances. This is why Shyamalan's script is sparse in terms of dialogue and contains numerous pauses between words, thus going against the formulaic structure repeatedly being used at present (the 'more is less' approach). He is aware the actors will fill these spaces with non-verbal actions and reactions and that the accumulation of these small details will help create fully rounded characters for the audience. In other words, body language 'speaks' to us as well as verbal language in this film and it cannot be conveyed in a short space of time, because this non-verbal language is something that takes time to read and recognise in real life. Shyamalan is not just joining the dots to get from event to event; he wants the audience to relate to the characters' emotional shifts. This is because **The Sixth Sense**, while styling itself as an old-school horror film, is not primarily concerned with frightening us; it is about a man trying to regain what he once had and a child facing his fears.

Another reason why the film has to be slow in terms of development is also to do with communication. Malcolm has to win Cole's trust in order to reveal his secret (in more ways than he is aware of, due to his ignorance of his own state), just as any child psychologist needs to, and to do this also takes time. Had Cole revealed it earlier in the narrative, the story would have lost credibility, as children do not reveal themselves to adults quickly. Shyamalan therefore has to show a number of 'sessions' between Malcolm and Cole with time-lapses in between; he has to build their opening up to each other by gradually saying things they would not have initially confided. That this also allows the director to build suspense and tension in keeping with a certain approach to the horror genre again reflects his skill as a scriptwriter. As Shyamalan has said:

> When you write something and then you listen to it, in your head, the empty spaces between the lines are really powerful… [if] you insinuate something, it comes out in brevity…[47]

In other words, Shyamalan is fully aware that

NOTES:

47 Argent, *Creative Screenwriting*, 1999.

true communication between the protagonists, and the difficulties they face in doing this, must be reflected in the script (and so the film) in order for the audience to recognise and appreciate that these characters – even if they appear 'different' (being able to see ghosts) or have gone through different experiences (being shot) – are still fundamentally just like us. Honest communication between ourselves and those we care about is not a continuous flow; unless said in anger, it is full of hesitation in order to see how the other person is reacting and/or to consider what we want to say next and the way we should say it. It contains pauses because we are often afraid to say what we need to, either because we are revealing ourselves or because we do not want to hurt the other. In **The Sixth Sense**, these pauses show that the characters are human. Cole may be a 'hyper-compassionate' boy (a condition supposedly common to mediums),[48] but he is still a boy. Shyamalan understands that children can be hurt by words in a way adults are not. Spectators who see this film may be themselves inarticulate, may themselves be hurt by words, but they are cognisant things can be said for a variety of reasons beyond that of a direct statement in itself and understand that children can be damaged by words in a way they are not. Shyamalan remembers that words do not just cut like a knife for children, they can be a snail crawling along a razorblade.

Malcolm's and Lynn's pauses between utterances with Cole reflect this understanding just as much as their dialogue with him. They pause before they speak in order to choose their words carefully because they know they are speaking to a child. Malcolm does it through his professional training (though the audience knows it is more than this); Lynn does it out of **love**.

Lynn's conflict between her love for Cole and her fears about his behaviour has already been explored in section two. What is of concern here is the way she reflects this conflict through how she communicates with him.

One of the (many) interesting discoveries that occur when revisiting this film is the realisation that Lynn is actually far more hesitant in communicating with her son than Cole is with his mother. Though it takes almost the entire film before Cole finally summons up the courage to tell his mother what he experiences, Cole answers questions previously asked by her truthfully and directly, even though he knows she will not like or accept the answers.[49] Cole may have developed avoidance strategies so as not to be considered a 'freak', as he puts it, but he only uses them when he knows honesty will cause further difficulties for him.

Lynn, though, not only hesitates asking the questions, she fails to ask him the ones that matter. As such, Cole and Lynn's family ties are disintegrating as much due to her as to him. Lynn is a woman who does not have much, but what she does have she is trying to control. She may be holding down two jobs, she may be a single parent, but as far as she is concerned, these things happen and you hold yourself together, no matter what. Her son's behaviour and emotional state, therefore, are not things she can easily identify with. That this state leads to him drawing a picture of a man stabbing someone else in the neck with a screwdriver, for example, is alien to her. As far as she is concerned, life is hard but whatever else you do, you cope – so she does not know how to deal with the fact that Cole's behaviour is spinning their life out of control. Though she knows Cole is troubled, she never really tries to find out why (only once does she ask him what is wrong, at a time when he is too upset to say anything). Even when she notices the unusual lights that appear in photographs of Cole, she never asks him about them or even points them out.

This hesitation in terms of her character is balanced by her love for her son, shown through the sequences of her talking in her sleep about defending Cole and her telephone call to the parents whose son she believes has injured him (subconsciously enforced by the fact she drives a Volvo, despite it not being the cheapest of cars to

NOTES:

48 During his research, Shyamalan discovered that children who said they talked to people who had passed away, or inexplicably knew of information, were overwhelmingly from single-parent families, no matter what their income bracket or social background. This is why Cole's father is completely absent and why Vincent mentions his parents had divorced in the film.

49 The one exception to this is the sequence where all the kitchen cabinets and drawers have been opened (specifically, four cupboard doors, five large and two small pull-out drawers on initial re-entry into the kitchen by Lynn, then nine drawers and seven doors in total as the camera pans around). When Lynn asks Cole what he was looking for, he hesitantly answers 'Pop Tarts'.

3. Themes and Characterisation

run). From these two moments, the audience learns that Lynn, as Shyamalan puts it, is 'a damn lioness, and she's ready to protect her child'.[50] However, it is precisely this behaviour that discretely explains why she fails to communicate with Cole just as much as he is unable to communicate with her. As a character, Lynn shows us she thinks in terms of binary opposites: it is one thing or the other. Either Cole injured himself or other children did it to him. The possibility of a third alternative does not enter her mind.

Fig. 6: Lynn talking in her sleep

Crowe and Anna's failure to communicate is of course understood completely by the audience by the end of the film: it is difficult to communicate with someone when you are dead. However, because we are not aware of this throughout the film, Shyamalan uses this failure of communication not only to build up to the twist, but to both explore his major theme in another direction and develop Crowe's character.

Malcolm as a character shows clear paradoxes right from the beginning of the film. We learn he is a successful child psychologist, which suggests he cares deeply about children (later confirmed by the 'bedtime story' quoted above), yet has none of his own. This is unusual for a psychologist of this sort and suggests either a desire to be a father or a character who experiences fatherhood vicariously through helping other children. Furthermore, while his profession is built on the ability to explore and talk with children about their emotional states, he cannot talk to his wife about his own (he only mentions to her once, very briefly, that he feels he is being given a 'second chance'). That none of this is explored in *The Sixth Sense* could

initially be laid at Shyamalan's door as a weakness in the script, but to do so would miss an essential point of Malcolm's character. The opening sequence of the film establishes that Malcolm is someone who needs no one else apart from Anna in his family unit because he is happy just as he is. This is why, in the script that was greenlighted, the last shot of *The Sixth Sense* ends with the video of Malcolm talking at his wedding using rhyming words: a reflection of the beginning of the film where he does the same. This Todorovian circularity was written for several reasons, but one of them is to expressly point out that Malcolm's love for Anna has not changed. He loves her just as much at the end of the film as he did at the beginning, and he loves her just as much at the beginning as he did when they got married. He wants and needs nothing else in his life but his wife and his job to bring him happiness.[51]

Malcolm therefore is a man who was not just physically wounded when shot by Vincent, he was figuratively wounded by his realisation that he failed to help this tortured man when he was a child. His happiness has been terminally (sic) altered, as his perfect world was suddenly and violently torn apart. This is why he searches for **redemption** through Cole. If he can redeem himself in terms of his work, he can become again the man he was – and so reclaim the life (and love) he had. The conflict within himself between finding redemption and holding onto his wife's love drives Malcolm's character, the story and audience empathy forward – and those spectators who notice that Malcolm wears the same clothes through most of the film can put it down to the fact that he no longer cares about anything except these two desires. Significantly, Shyamalan even explores at one point in the film Malcolm's consideration that if he cannot achieve both, he must achieve one. Malcolm chooses his wife, further consolidating that his love of Anna is the most important thing in his life (thus possibly explaining part of this film's appeal to older women, as its discrete 'confirmation' that their husband's or partner's love for them is also the most important thing is comforting).

NOTES:

50 Argent, ibid, 1999.

51 This scripted version of the ending was filmed, but Shyamalan had to reluctantly alter it - not because of its content, but because of the way he approached it. 'When we put the film together, it felt like two endings... because of the way I directed it, [it] came off as really sad; it wasn't the right note to end with, because neither Anna or Malcolm is feeling that at that moment'. Argent, ibid, 1999.

Malcolm cannot communicate with his wife, but he does not know this. As such, Shyamalan is able to explore how husbands fail to communicate with wives due to their misunderstanding of what women want to hear and what they think women want to hear. Crowe is a wonderful representation of a sensitive man who is nevertheless a man. He tries to explain his inattentiveness as a husband through the importance of his work rather than trying to explain *why* he is working so hard. For Malcolm it is because of his need for redemption, but this need is a metaphor for the adult audience, both male and female. The committed male spectator can replace it with his own individual needs, whatever those needs may be. The female can understand that their male partners may not express themselves fully because of the separation in their minds of what they do and what they feel. Shyamalan both recognises the male fear of losing control (Malcolm's inability to hold Anna to him when faced with the need to work combined with a younger man's attention to his wife that appears to be semi-reciprocated) and the female fear of being unappreciated (Anna's seeming deep hurt that he forgets an important celebration of their love).

What Shyamalan also recognises is that women want affirmation – that what is being done is done, at least partly, out of love for them. That Malcolm and Anna have no children emphasises this point; it seems Malcolm has been so affected by the dramatic events that have occurred to him he has forgotten the most important thing: his marriage to a woman whom he loves and who loves him. As such, the young writer/director reflects fundamental concerns of an older audience as well as a younger one.

It is interesting to note that the screen time devoted to the exploration of certain themes does not imply a hierarchical order, which again reflects the hidden subtleties of this film. For example, Malcolm's relationship with his wife, despite it taking up less screen time than Cole's relationship with his mother, is actually more complicated (though perhaps less powerful in a

dramatic sense) in terms of the theme being explored. Even when we do discover Malcolm has been losing Anna because he has died, rather than a breakdown of their relationship due to his being shot and the subsequent need for redemption, the emphasis is not just on the audience's reinterpretation of the events that have occurred beforehand. It also contains a reflection of the nature of love and loss. Paradoxically, Shyamalan had to cut a significant amount of the video seen right at the end of the film in order to achieve this, as originally it emphasised Malcolm's pain in terms of what he once had, rather than his understanding and acceptance of why he no longer has it.

Of the four main characters in the film, Anna's is the most sparing. She appears to be in mourning, which of course we subsequently discover is the case, but during the film it seems this mourning is over a disintegrating marriage. It is also suggested that she is contemplating having and perhaps actually begins an adulterous affair with Sean (Glenn Fitzgerald), who works for her. Anna therefore runs the risk of being seen in an unsympathetic light by members of the audience, but this is counterbalanced by Sean's character. He is younger than her, a little awkward, sweet and innocent. He is portrayed as having more a crush on Anna than sexual intentions. In this way, it is understandable that she feels something for him.

The most apparent exploration of the theme of communication is between Cole and the ghosts that plague him. The boy lives in a world only he can see and that world is frightening. Though he finds solace in a church and the tent in his bedroom that he has filled with stolen religious artefacts, even these are invaded – the former by Malcolm, though we are not aware of it at the time; the latter by Kyra, the ghost Cole finally listens to.[52] Cole lives in fear every moment of his waking life, and this fear and his 'hyper-compassionate' ability lead to an estrangement from his mother and being ostracised by his peers. This is why he says more than once, 'De profundis clamavi ad te, Domine'.[53] He is not

NOTES:

52 Except of course she isn't, as Cole has been previously listening to Crowe.

53 'Out of the depths, I cry to you, O Lord' (Psalm 129).

3. Themes and Characterisation

Fig 7: "I'm ready to communicate with you now."(© BFI Stills)

just repeating a supplication he has heard from a ghost, it is a prayer of his own.

Malcolm's suggestion that, rather than trying to hide from them, Cole communicates with these ghosts by listening to what they want to say and help them 'move on' (and in doing so, no longer haunt him) is the key that allows Cole to face and overcome his fear. This results in his healing the rift between Lynn and his actualisation of peer (and teacher) acceptance. In fact, this communication with the ghosts, which in itself results from his finally 'connecting' with Malcolm, leads to subsequent communication. Now that he understands and accepts why they haunt him and so is no longer frightened by them, whatever their appearance, Cole has the courage to communicate with his mother.[54] However, to communicate is not the same as convince and so Shyamalan beautifully uses two different types of communication in order to achieve this (thus bringing resolution in respect to this sub-plot). The first is Cole finally telling his mother what it is he experiences; the second is his communicating a 'message' from Lynn's own mother about seeing her dance and how proud she is of her daughter. Cole therefore does not just communicate himself, he passes on another communication that covertly suggests another ghost is able to rest.

With Cole's eventual communication with the dead, Shyamalan sends his central thematic message home to the audience: if you speak your fears, you can overcome them. In this film, communication is the key to healing yourself and others. This is why Vincent, who is too afraid to reveal his secret, dies through his own hand and why Cole not only survives, but triumphs. It is no coincidence the leading role Cole plays in the second school production is that of King Arthur as a boy.[55] As Harty obliquely explored when analysing **The Sixth Sense** from a specific point of view, in Arthurian legend Arthur will 'heal' the land and the people as the 'once and future' king.[56] The boy-king here returns as Cole, who can draw the sword from the stone because he has accepted the authority that previously frightened him so much. Cole not only heals himself, he heals Malcolm; not just by being the conduit for Malcolm's redemption, but also by suggesting to Malcolm he should talk to Anna while she is asleep. Cole therefore helps Malcolm in the same way that Malcolm helped him; each of them finds the solution to the other's anguish. Cole also heals his mother both in terms of his relationship with her and in terms of Lynn's relationship with her (dead) mother. By revealing his ability, as he now sees it, Cole not only takes the first step to rebuilding their relationship, but through telling his mother what his grandmother wants to say, he heals both a pain his mother has never let go of and a fear she now has. Lynn was not able to attend Cole's leading role in the play, just as her own mother – she thought – did not see her dance. Cole eases her guilt by revealing the cycle has already been broken. Lynn's mother did see her dance, so she is not following in her footsteps. As such, Shyamalan is saying to the older audience: you may think you are becoming your parents, but you are not.

The Arthurian legend is followed further. Cole is the once and future king because he connects the past (the dead who are themselves haunted by events when they were alive) and the future (for himself, his mother and for Malcolm, who by learning he can now let go and move on to the 'afterlife' represents all the ghosts who can do the same through Cole). Malcolm therefore becomes Merlin to Cole's Arthur; a magical guide (in that he is supernatural) who helps the boy realise he has a special role to play: he has been given a gift

NOTES:

54 Emphasised, perhaps too much, by Cole using the opening line, 'I'm ready to communicate with you now'. Shyamalan (or Toni Collette) may have become aware of this though and so Lynn semi-queries the use of this word, resulting in the audience putting it down to Cole's exposure to Malcolm's use of terminology.

55 The first school production appears to be a stage adaptation of *The Jungle Book* (1967), again about a boy who is 'different', in that he can talk to animals.

56 Harty, *Arthuriana*, 2000.

of healing tortured souls. This is why Cole looks to Malcolm and Malcolm nods to Cole to remove the sword before he does so. Malcolm has passed on his own 'gift' to the boy, that of listening to and helping those in despair. The only difference is that Malcolm helped the living and Cole helps the dead. Even Cole's surname (Sear) reflects this gift. He is indeed a 'seer' of things we cannot and, as a result, is able to do something the vast majority of us are not able to do. Through the metaphor of seeing – and subsequently communicating with – the dead, Shyamalan is implicitly telling the audience that we too can be like Cole. We too can choose to heal ourselves; we too can help others to heal. All of us can pull the sword from the stone, because we are all capable of being 'pure of heart', if we only connect through true communication.

Fig. 8: Cole pulls the sword from the stone

The themes of **death** and the nature of **mortality** are explored through the ghosts themselves and why they are such. All of these spirits cannot move on because they feel there is something in their life that was left unresolved. For Malcolm, it is not just the need for redemption but to tell his wife she was the most important thing in his life, that she was 'never second' (which Anna expressed to him at the beginning of the film). For Kyra it is the need to tell her father she was poisoned by her mother and through this save her sister who, it is inferred, the mother is now also poisoning. However, on one level these two characters are merely reflecting a fear we all have: that we may die suddenly leaving things undone and unsaid. The fear of this type of death – one that does not allow for closure; does not allow us to say goodbye to our loved ones or tell them how much we love them – haunts us more and

more as we get older and gain more responsibilities. As Shyamalan described it:

> … somebody stabs you and wants your money. You're dying on the sidewalk… and you're yelling I have to pick up my kid at three, my wife's not here yet. You have a million open-ended things… If his family was there, he might have been able to go in peace because he could have said, are you going to be all right? And they would have said, we'll be all right, Pops.[57]

The anxiety the spectator feels about this type of death, and the knowledge that we are mortal and will all die at some point, is temporarily allayed by the end of *The Sixth Sense*. Life may be fragile, but there is something else after it, signified by Malcolm disappearing in a blaze of pure white light. Mars-Jones criticised this ending when he wrote 'nothing could be more American, and more kitsch, than this vision of the afterlife. No God, no judgement, just guardian angels and healing'.[58] However, Shyamalan has to end the film on this upbeat note: had he faded to black the audience would have been unsure what will happen to Malcolm (and so ourselves) now that he has found closure and no longer needs to stay. To have ended the film with some angelic figure dressed in white welcoming him would have been far more kitsch and clichéd. Shyamalan precisely does *not* show guardian angels; he does not even show a guardian ghost. Malcolm is there to help Cole, not protect him. Shyamalan therefore leaves the ending deliberately abstract; each member of the audience can interpret the white light in whatever way they see fit. It is left to us to 'fill in the blank'.

Shyamalan has said he likes horror films that are 'a little bit spiritual, and that have some meaning. It should be a decent ride'.[59] The themes of *The Sixth Sense* do not dominate the film, as the director knows of paramount importance when making a commercial movie is that the audience is entertained. However, through his subtle development of the characters, Shyamalan explores themes that concern us all, while making sure the audience get a very decent ride indeed.

NOTES:

57 Nocenti, *Scenario*, 2001.

58 Mars-Jones, *The Times*, 1999.

59 Nocenti, ibid, 2001.

4. Film Language

This section will primarily deal with cinematography, sound, editing and *mise-en-scène*. *Mise-en-scène* literally means 'putting into the scene', but is now used to refer to the look of the film; in other words everything seen by the audience within the framed shot. It is concerned with the setting (including the film's props and location), the lighting, the costume and make-up, and the movement of the figures (including blocking and any special effects to do with movement, human or otherwise). More than this, though, it will also consider *The Sixth Sense*'s particular use of motifs and horror genre iconography. Scarratt defines iconography as 'any cultural image which has powerful resonance, or which encapsulates or embodies an aspect of culture or an idea'.[60] What will be explored is how this film uses iconography and motifs, 'borrowing' one of them in particular, while also creating new ones. However, the film's use of some of these motifs is unusual in that, rather than being 'read' and understood by the spectator on initial viewing, they are meant to be recognised (indeed searched for) on subsequent viewings. As such, they are both present and hidden within the film. On this level, *The Sixth Sense* becomes a visual puzzle that challenges the audience to find all the references.

The film is set in **Philadelphia**, Shyamalan's hometown and where he still continues to live. In fact the entire film was shot there, including the seven studio sets, which were constructed inside Philadelphia's old Civic Center where the production was based. However, this does not mean Shyamalan could have filmed *The Sixth Sense* anywhere. Had he lived in New York or Chicago, he could not have made the film there, because these cities would not have reflected the tone of the film. Shyamalan presents Philadelphia as a *quiet* place. The exterior shots do not have honking taxis or streets filled with people; cats do not howl and dogs do not bark (except the one owned by the Sears, but at night he only whimpers). Everyone except Malcolm seems to be indoors by the time it gets dark.

Moreover, the Philadelphia Shyamalan depicts is not strictly speaking the tourist version. While some of the city's more impressive architecture is seen, its most celebrated monuments and artefacts (the Liberty Bell, for example) are not. Instead, he concentrates on a Philadelphia that shows the type of place it is – a sturdy, ordered, well-maintained historical city – that works as a backdrop for the storyline. As such, it reflects the film itself: a carefully planned and constructed, tightly plotted old-fashioned type of horror movie that contains no excess(ive) padding. The film-maker does not need to emphasise the city's history, it is present through the shots of the streets and the buildings. Shyamalan shows a Philadelphia that is safe, tidy, almost homely – which emphasises how unsafe and alienated Cole feels.

There are no drunks, pushers, pimps, drug addicts or prostitutes in Shyamalan's Philadelphia, because this is a place where the present inhabitants are respectfully aware of the city's past. Cole's school was once a courthouse where colonial corpses were hung; Derrick's birthday party is held in a house where a servant died after being locked up in a small cupboard. As Shyamalan says, 'You can't walk down a street or pass a house or school in Philly without wondering who lived there and who died there… it's steeped in so much history.'[61] No wonder Cole is visited by so many ghosts. This city is *old* (well, old for America); there are a lot of ghosts around.

Most of the location shots were filmed in old Philadelphia, but new parts of the city were also used. While it is the older buildings that stand out (the City Hall, the Undine Barge Club on Boat House Row, Old St. Augustine's Church, Head House Square, Pierce College, the St. Albans Court neighbourhood, and residences and shops along Pine, Walnut, Broad, Chestnut, Delancey and Mt. Vernon Streets), newer ones

---

NOTES:

60 Scarratt, *Science Fiction Film: A Teacher's Guide to the Genre*, 2001.

61 Source unknown.

are used effectively (the Presbyterian Medical Center and the Striped Bass restaurant).

Tak Fujimoto, the film's cinematographer, does not just bring out a city steeped in the past, though. Shyamalan chose him because of his work on *Silence of the Lambs* (1991). 'For ***The Sixth Sense***, I knew I wanted a kind of heightened realism, but one that really stayed as grounded to reality as possible in the visual approach', which he felt Fujimoto had achieved in that film.[62] However, the fact the cinematographer had filmed in the city before, on ***Philadelphia*** (1993) and ***Beloved*** (1998), was no doubt an advantage in terms of working with the crew. Fujimoto seems to have kept the suspense of each sequence at the forefront through framing, camera movement, blocking of scenes and particularly lighting. He and production designer Larry Fulton use a very muted, de-saturated palette (whites, creams, tans, browns, pale blues and greys). The interiors, for example, are downplayed in terms of colours. All of this was done for a specific purpose – to highlight the **red** objects that punctuate the film.

The colour red appears throughout the film. It occurs not just in terms of the setting, but also in respect to props and costume. It is the colour of the church doors, the doorknob to the basement, the balloon and the carpet on the stairs at the party, Anna's anti-depressants, her dress at the anniversary dinner, the shawl she wears at home whenever Malcolm is present and the napkin she uses when eating alone. Cole wears a red sweater and it is the colour of his tent (deliberately accentuated by the flashlight Cole uses within it). Kyra's mother wears an entirely inappropriate red dress and has red lipstick on at the funeral of her daughter; Lynn is wearing a red sweater when the dead cyclist appears; Sean's present is wrapped in red tissue. When Malcolm is outside in daylight, the red bricks of Philadelphia can always be seen and Cole's school is red because of the ghosts that are constantly present. As Malcolm and Cole, in the background, walk up a red-paved sidewalk, children wearing red baseball caps walk by and there is a red stop sign in the mid-

ground. Cole's free-association writing, in which he writes down what he hears from the dead, is done in red ink.

Fig. 9: Mrs. Barton wears red at her daughter's funeral... an unusual colour choice

Red of course is a clue that denotes a ghost is present, even though some clues can still be missed despite repeated viewings. For example, after seeing Malcolm sitting across from his apartment in the sequence when they first meet, Cole hurriedly walks past red-bricked buildings, red-painted steps and red flowers, then runs past red-brick, red patched and red painted walls before entering the church with the red doors where, after speaking to Malcolm, he steals a religious artefact dominantly painted red. The spectator may have noticed all of these references through close observation, but how many of them would have registered that the curtains on the door of Cole's apartment building initially appear to be red at the very moment he first notices Malcolm? When he closes it, they change colour due to the light. Similarly, in the hospital sequence where Dr Hill (Shyamalan himself) speaks to Lynn about Cole's 'suspicious' cuts and bruises, the colour red is used far more subtly (the sweater worn by an extra holding a baby in the background; the red letters above Malcolm's head). However, there are times when it is not used, such as when Malcolm is sitting with Lynn waiting for Cole to return from school.[63]

Apart from this expressionistic use of red, Shyamalan and Fujimoto tried to keep the film's look naturalistic. They did not, for example, use blue lights in Cole's hallway when ghosts appear – a device commonly employed in horror films to

---

NOTES:

62 Holborn, *American Images*, 2000.

63 However, she has red nail-polish on and is sitting on the only orange chair in the room - so perhaps that counts.

4. Film Language

visually heighten the fear and tension due to its cold, harsh appearance – but kept to the lighting conditions people would actually see in these types of hallway. Neither do their ghosts have a supernatural glow or emit an ethereal light; in fact on one occasion (Cole's make-up woman) we are not initially aware she is even a ghost.

Fig. 10: Cole and the 'make-up ghost'

Apart from the above-mentioned use of red, costume is also important in respect to Malcolm Crowe. Willis's clothing had to be meticulously selected so that it appeared slightly different in respect to various types of lighting. Depending on the lighting conditions, the colour of the material alters subtly. Sometimes it appears grey, sometimes greyish-brown or greyish-blue. The idea behind this was that, though Willis wears the same clothes throughout the film, they did not look exactly the same and as such it was hoped the audience would not notice a 'clue' to Crowe's actual (non) physical state.[64] Joanna Johnston, the film's costume designer, also ensured that all the characters appeared in relatively nondescript clothing in terms of colour (browns, umbers, blacks, pale blues and lilacs), again to heighten the red objects.

Another device used in the film is that of **shadows**. Shadows are a common device used in the horror genre to enhance the mood, including – as it is done here – emphasising those cast by figures through lighting techniques so that they appear elongated. A number of sequences contain shots of a character's shadow showing their actions in silhouette form and shadows in general are accentuated, particularly Cole's. An example of this is when Cole enters Kyra's bedroom. We do not see him to begin with, but rather watch his shadow move over her videos and toys before his hand reaches out to select one; it is only after this that we get a shot of Cole standing in the room. Another example is how Anna and Malcolm first become aware of Vincent's presence in their home; his shadow passes over them. However, Shyamalan also uses the idea of shadow in a way that horror genre films have rarely, if ever, done previously. The sequences in which Malcolm appears were carefully developed to ensure he did not cast a shadow, another of the clues in *The Sixth Sense*. Except for a prominent one at the beginning of the movie when he was still alive, Malcolm is the only major character who consistently does not cast a shadow, although it was not always possible – which is why Malcolm's shadow can occasionally be seen if one studies the film carefully enough. However, this is so brief and infrequent it was decided it was not worth the cost of digitally removing it.

Shadows are also used to heighten the film's atmosphere. Because the exterior location shots at night are so devoid of people, some of these locations feel distinctly eerie. This eeriness is emphasised even further due to their being shot so late at night. Several shots were filmed at two in the morning; as a result the shadows cast on the cobblestones, caused by cascading ivy, give the city an almost otherworldly look.

A third device that appears several times in *The Sixth Sense* is that of **reflections**, through the use of mirrors (Crowe watching his wife taking a shower in the mirrored door of the bathroom cabinet) and glass (Malcolm and Anna's reflections in the framed citation). Reflection in film is often a visual signifier to show a separation or distancing between characters and Shyamalan uses it in precisely this way. In respect to the glassed citation, it is done as a premonitory device of what is to come. As we see their reflection in it, Malcolm says, 'We should hang it in the bathroom' – the very place where Vincent will fire the gun that terminally distances the couple. The bathroom mirror emphasises the distance Malcolm knows has grown between himself and

NOTES:

64 In fact he does not. He also wears the grey 'Varsity' sweatshirt (with red lettering) Anna handed to him the night he was shot both when Sean first calls on his wife and when Cole tells him his secret.

his wife. He looks but feels he cannot touch anymore. Anna is too far away; she is barely speaking to him and taking anti-depressants. Reflections also appear on other occasions to convey different meanings; for example, when Cole and Crowe travel on a bus in order to attend Kyra's funeral. The audience sees Cole sitting next to a window from outside the bus for part of the scene and the buildings Cole looks at are reflected in the glass. Cole's way of looking suggests he is seeing more than just bricks and mortar, emphasised when he sits back rapidly after seeing a cemetery. Similarly, Cole's reflection in the doorknob to Kyra's bedroom again suggests he is aware the room contains more than just objects. That Malcolm is not seen in this reflection, despite the fact the audience has just seen him standing behind Cole, is yet another clue as to Malcolm's actual state. The picture behind Malcolm is clearly seen both on the wall and in the doorknob's reflection. Malcolm, however, has disappeared.

There is a prop that appears prominently only once, but it is an important one. It is the **light bulb** shown at the very beginning of the film. The shot of this bulb being turned on represents, for Shyamalan, that moment between light and dark when the spirits leave a space and the living enter it. This is why it is shown in slow motion, one of only two slow motion shots in the film.[65] The film-maker is making a symbolic statement about the content of *The Sixth Sense*; this film will explore a world in which the seen and the unseen – the physical and the spiritual – both exist.

Fig. 11: The light bulb, the moment between light and dark

The special effects in *The Sixth Sense* distinctly owe more to contemporary horror films than classical ones. Nothing is particularly suggested here. We see the cut wrists, the burn victim, the cyclist killed in the road accident. However, these effects are more old-school than new. They are achieved through make-up and costume rather than computer-generated imagery. Furthermore, they are not dwelt on as is often the case in the contemporary horror genre. We sometimes only glimpse these graphic details; others we see just long enough for us to register what has happened to the victim. Kyra's vomiting is gruesome, but it is not projectile and it certainly does not cover Cole and his tent. Also, Shyamalan deliberately avoids showing how these victims died. The hung corpses are not shown strangling; the beaten wife is not shown cutting her wrists. Even Malcolm being shot and Vincent killing himself are downplayed. The blood from Malcolm's exit wound does not splatter the walls and Vincent's suicide is not seen, only heard (this nevertheless shows an understanding of contemporary audiences' aural expectations; we do not just hear a gunshot but the blood hitting the bathroom interior). In other words, the graphic special effects film-makers tend to use to attract the 15 to 24-year-olds, the largest single audience demographic in terms of box-office return accounting for approximately 60% of the total cinema-going public, are not used here. The only death specified in this film is Kyra's poisoning and there is no gore present, which indeed makes it far more shocking. The poisoning by her mother is done casually, as a matter of course. It brings home a horror no amount of visceral detail can do; this is a murderous act that does occur and this is how it is done – pragmatically, in a measured, calculated way and with no emotion whatsoever. The fact we see this act on video emphasises this distancing. Kyra's mother sees what she is doing in a detached way; she monitors Kyra's slow death just as a camera would.

Another special effect used extensively in the film is also a motif in the same way as the colour red. However, unlike Shyamalan's original use of red, this one is knowingly 'borrowed'.

NOTES:

65 The other is when Lynn carries Cole out of the small cupboard he becomes trapped in at the party.

4. Film Language

Shyamalan has said in several interviews that one of the films he most admires and been influenced by is *The Exorcist*. The visual representation of a sudden drop in temperature through the characters' **cold breath** in *The Sixth Sense* is therefore not only a motif in itself, it is also an intertextual reference or at the very least an homage to this film.[66] If this particular special effect had been used in the horror films previously, it was certainly not used to such effect as it was in *The Exorcist*, and that film established it as an iconographic visual image in terms of the genre. However, in *The Exorcist* the drop in temperature was linked to possession, whereas in *The Sixth Sense* it signifies the presence of ghosts. Shyamalan therefore has taken this motif and subverted it. He knows the audience is at least subconsciously aware of what it signifies, so deliberately uses it for different ends. As such, when the spectator becomes sentient that temperature drops are appearing at the times ghosts appear, they are also unknowingly witnessing a transition in genre iconography.

In terms of blocking (the movement of the actors into, out of and within the frame), Shyamalan often uses the tried-and-tested approach of having figures suddenly appear from the side of the screen close-up (though on one occasion a figure does it in the background). However, these figures do not jump into view but rather glide in. The actors move almost as if they are not taking steps, but floating across the floor, entirely in keeping with audience perceptions of how ghosts should move, in part due to how they have been depicted in previous horror films. Again, though, Shyamalan uses this convention in a slightly different way. His ghosts do not float above the ground; they float on it. This impression is only partly caused through actor movement; another factor in achieving this is that the ghosts' legs rarely appear in the frame as they move and when they do it is in the background and slightly out of focus.

Along with these particular aspects of *mise-en-scène*, there are other lesser ones, but they are worth pointing out briefly due to their repeated appearance in Shyamalan's other films. They include fluttering curtains (when Anna discovers the broken window), car accidents (when Cole reveals his secret to his mother), the use of water to signify death or weakness (Vincent shoots Malcolm while standing in the bathroom), important sequences in basements (Crowe hears the ghosts whispering to Vincent on tape, which convinces him Cole is telling the truth), shots of and through leaves and windows (in the latter case, this also includes protagonists framed within them), red-haired women who deliver important thematic messages in each film (Lynn telling Cole 'If we can't talk to each other, we're not gonna make it') and, though not strictly speaking *mise-en-scène*, cameo appearances by the writer/ director. The use of one or two dominant colours has also repeatedly occurred in Shyamalan's films.

Cinematography means 'writing in movement'. It is concerned with how what is being filmed works in terms of light, tone and colour and does so primarily in three ways: the framing, the duration and the photographic aspects of the shot. *The Sixth Sense* appears to have been filmed with a mixture of low contrast, slow film stock (which gives gentle, blended images) and high contrast, slow film stock (which gives bright highlights and dark areas, but still in a gentle way). Apart from the previously mentioned emphasis of shadows (or lack of) cast by the characters, light and shadow in general are not sharply defined because in Cole's world the living and the dead intermingle. The dark corners are not emphasised in this film because the 'monsters' do not need to hide there waiting to attack the victim. They are all around him, even in the middle of the day. The audience therefore sees a similar world; one in which the 'real' and the 'unreal' are not clearly separate. Cole can stand in a brightly lit school corridor and see hanging corpses – and he can talk to a ghost while doing so.

Shyamalan uses a range of framing devices and camera movements, but there are three that

---

NOTES:

66 'Intertextuality' is a postmodern term to refer to a 'text' (in this case a film) that consciously refers to one or more previous 'texts' in its own construction - e.g. Lynch's references to *The Wizard of Oz* (1939) in his film *Wild at Heart* (1990).

particularly stand out. The first is his use of the **hand-held camera** at moments of dramatic intensity. As many of these moments are intended to be unnerving or frightening, the director and cinematographer enhance this experience for the spectator visually through this approach. The protagonists' world is not stable at these times, so it does not appear stable to us. However, this camera work is as far from that used in *The Blair Witch Project* as it is from the Steadicam use in *The Shining*. Just as we do in the real world when something scares us, Shyamalan is trying to make us jump, not keep running. Hand-held shots, when kept as steady as possible, will still be unsteady, but they will not be out of kilter or show blurred movements. The film-maker wants us to feel uncomfortable, to suggest something *could* go very wrong, not that something already has. So the hand-held camera gives each of these moments a visual edginess in order to further engender a feeling of fear and unease in the audience.

The second is his use of 'bird's-eye view' and **overhead camera** angles. These shots from directly above occur several times in the film – the most prominent being when Malcolm is shot. The film cuts to an overhead shot of Malcolm lying on the bed and gradually pulls back as he holds his hands to his stomach before fading to black. An overhead shot such as this can be read as a visual suggestion of the spirit leaving the body. Another noticeable occurrence is when Malcolm leans against the wall at the end of the film. The film cuts to Anna breathing, then back to a close-up shot of Malcolm. It appears he is still leaning against the wall, but then the camera pulls back and we see Malcolm directly from above, again lying on his bed. This is a visual transition, achieved through the pattern of the wallpaper being similar to the pattern on the pillow.

The third cinematographic device Shyamalan uses for particular effect is that of the **slow pan**. It occurs most prominently in the sequence where Lynn asks Cole why he keeps taking the bumble-bee pendant. The sequence was filmed in

Fig 12: Cole and Lynn at the table (© BFI Stills)

one take and begins with a wide two-shot of Cole and Lynn sitting at the kitchen table. As their conversation increases in tension, the camera slowly pushes in. When Lynn asks her son about the pendant, the camera pans slightly, eliminating Cole from the frame, and continues pushing in on her. As they continue talking, the camera slowly pans from mother to son, but still pushes in. As a result, the pans between the two characters increase in length so that, as they speak, the audience sees more of the space between them than the characters themselves. The slow panning is therefore a device that visually emphasises the discomfort Cole and Lynn are feeling during the conversation and enhances the tension between them. More than this, though, by spending so much time on the space between the two, it reflects the breakdown of Cole and Lynn's relationship; they too are becoming increasingly distant from each other.

The use of **sound** in *The Sixth Sense* is noticeable as much for its absence as its presence. This silence or quietening of surrounding ambient noise heightens the audience's awareness of small sounds: a door opening, floorboards creaking, the lifting of a box lid that contains Kyra's video or the siren heard in the distance as Malcolm walks

NOTES:

home. However, some of these **diegetic** sounds (sounds heard by the audience that come from a source in the story-world) are not just emphasised by the surrounding silence, but through the use of **acoustic foreground** – an artificial increase in volume in order to bring a particular sound to the spectator's attention. The sound of people breathing, in particular exhalation, is focused on in respect to this film. This is not just done in relation to people breathing while in the presence of ghosts, but breathing generally. The sound of the characters' breath while they are moving or even just sitting can be heard throughout the film, perhaps to suggest that everywhere, in every room, spirits are present. Another diegetic sound emphasised in *The Sixth Sense* is that of leaves rustling in the trees (see also below), again used to enhance the ghostly atmosphere. The movement of these leaves by the wind, however, is not just achieved through a slight heightening of acoustic foreground; it is also done through the lessening in volume of other exterior sounds so that it stands out.

Shyamalan also manipulates the characters' dialogue in terms of **sound bridging**. This mainly occurs with dialogue from a scene still continuing as it visually fades out, done in order to carry resonance into the next, but on some occasions the dialogue begun in one scene finishes after we have cut to the next or starts before we have cut to the new scene. At one point we see a flashback in terms of the film's story but continue to hear dialogue from the present time (Malcolm talking to Cole about free association writing) and at another we hear dialogue from a later scene (Malcolm telling Cole he cannot be his doctor anymore) aurally superimposed on the one before it (Malcolm 'breaking' the glass of Anna's shop door). Shyamalan of course also uses dialogue flashbacks in the final sequence as Malcolm interprets Cole's words in a new light regarding his own existence. However, on the whole, *The Sixth Sense* is straightforward in terms of its use of sound. Most of the sound heard is **onscreen diegetic** sound (the spectator sees what is making the sound on the screen) and most of the **offscreen**

diegetic sound (sounds created by diegetic sources that the audience do not see) is background noise. Similarly, all of the dialogue is **external diegetic** sound, in that it is heard by characters onscreen – or in terms of the ghosts, one other character in the form of Cole – as well as the audience.[67] **Internal diegetic** sound (when the spectator hears a character voicing thoughts the other characters do not hear) does not occur in the film, as even in the denouement Malcolm is not voicing his thoughts, but remembering Cole's previously spoken words.

The understated use of diegetic sound is complemented by the use of **non-diegetic** sound (sounds heard by the audience that do not come from a source in the story-world). The soundtrack of *The Sixth Sense* is orchestral and manages to be both highly atmospheric while also having overtones of the 'old-school' approach to scoring horror films with its emphasis on violins and strings. However, having said this, the film relies on creating ambience as much through electronic as orchestral means. The use of a sound motif in the form of a simple refrain on the piano is heard throughout the film, but there is a second that sounds distinctly synthesised and the film does have an Electronic Score Production credit for J.T. Hill. There is also a third musical motif that combines piano, strings, a woodwind instrument and a trumpet (or their electronic equivalents). Contemporary music is overtly heard only once in this film, at the party Cole is invited to, which is understandable in that a child's birthday party is highly unlikely not to have it. Other than this, it does not seem to appear either diegetically or non-diegetically. At the beginning of the sequence where Cole reveals his secret to his mother, for example, not one driver has the radio on or is listening to music. However, this is not the case. Shyamalan actually sneaks in another form of contemporary music that reflects a very different Philadelphia 'tradition': the 'Philadelphia Sound'. It is heard in the background of a segment of the wedding video Malcolm watches while Anna is taking a shower upstairs, but is done so unobtrusively that the

NOTES:

67 Although, in Malcolm's case, it is actually two - as Anna does 'hear' him talking to her while asleep.

68 There are actually six 'popular' recordings heard in the film in total and one classical piece in the form of Franz Schubert's Piano Quintet in A Major D667, 'Trout' Andante.

36   **FILM LANGUAGE** | *The Sixth Sense*

audience barely even notices it. However, this reference is actually ironic (or a mistake), as the song is *Come See About Me* by The Supremes, which was a Motown release![68] This lack of contemporary music is unusual in terms of horror films today, as it means the film's soundtrack can only be sold on its own merit, rather than a collection of songs likely to appeal to the film's younger audience.

In terms of **editing**, it has already been pointed out that *The Sixth Sense*, with only minor exceptions, follows the principles of classical continuity editing (p.9). It has also previously been explored how Shyamalan and Andrew Mondshein, the film's editor, often use multiple cuts in one sequence followed by few (or no) cuts in the next in order to create sleights-of-hand in respect to hiding the film's twist (p.12-13). However, there are other deviations from the standard editing approach. To begin with, though there are numerous points in the film where time passes between events the audience has just seen and the events they see next, there are no dissolves in this film. This is not particularly unusual in itself, but rather what replaces it. *The Sixth Sense* has a considerable amount of fade-outs and fade-ins; more than is usual in standard Hollywood fare. This is done not just to show the passing of time, but also to infer that this passing of time is ambiguous. In effect, the **temporal relation** between each scene (the time that has passed between one scene and another) is frequently not specified, giving the film's otherwordly feel further emphasis. At the end of the sequence when Cole decides to communicate with Kyra, there is almost a six second gap between the fade-to-black from this scene and the fade-in to Cole and Crowe travelling to Kyra's funeral. A one second fade-to-black is considered a long time in terms of a film's pace; to have this much negative space between two sequences should suggest that years have passed between the events. However this cannot be the case, as the funeral gathering must by necessity be occurring relatively shortly after Kyra's death. Therefore, Shyamalan and Mondshein are (yet again) subverting the

conventions of classical continuity editing; they are not primarily using the fades to suggest temporal shifts, they are doing it to emphasise the importance of events. In other words, Shyamalan is subliminally informing the audience that time is not important in terms of this film's narrative flow, because ghosts do not have a sense of time (which is why Malcolm tells Anna – but is actually telling us – that he keeps losing track of it). The more important the event, the longer the fade-to-black.

This ambiguity is still played with even when a straight cut is made from scene to scene. Cuts are usually done to suggest that the two sequences are occurring one after the other within a relatively short time-span, but in *The Sixth Sense* the temporal relations between cuts are still uncertain. Though some scenes clearly have close temporal proximity, others are far more vague. They could have occurred hours, days or weeks between each other. For example, the amount of time that passes between Malcolm telling Cole he can no longer work with him, Malcolm's listening to the tape of the session with Vincent and his subsequent seeking out of Cole in church appear to occur in a day, a night and the following day. But if Malcolm has decided to no longer work with Cole, why would he be listening to the tape that night? The answer of course is Malcolm is unable to start rebuilding his relationship with Anna, but we do not know that at this point in the film. In reality, even if we do change our minds about a choice we have made and decide to return to the one we rejected, we would at least spend some time pursuing the choice initially decided on. Malcolm chose his relationship over the case; as such he would not have returned to the case so soon. This cut is therefore misleading in terms of time; the events are not as close as they initially appear.

Shyamalan has said on a number of occasions when being interviewed that he has cracked Steven Spielberg's 'formula' to successful film-making, but refuses to reveal what it is. This allusion has often been interpreted as referring to

NOTES:

narrative and character development: for example, Spielberg's use of an opening sequence that begins slowly, then builds in terms of tension and action to a powerful climax, followed by a scene that not only gives the audience breathing space but is also important in terms of building at least one protagonist's character. Spielberg did this in *Jaws* (1975), *Close Encounters of the Third Kind* (1977), *Raiders of the Lost Ark* (1981) and *E.T. the Extra-Terrestrial* (1982). *The Sixth Sense* follows a similar approach in terms of its opening sequence: a slow start in the first minute (how much slower can you get than a slow-motion shot of a light-bulb being switched on and a selection of a bottle of wine?) that leads to a shocking conclusion (the film's 'star' is shot) – and Shyamalan has done the same with several of his other films, though arguably with less impact than he achieved with this one. Similarly, the two directors have similar approaches in terms of the traits and experiences the characters in their films have. There are a number of comparisons, one being that they often depict families where one parent is absent, either through separation or death; another is that their films contain children who are touched in some way by the extraordinary and the miraculous. Furthermore, both directors use 'fantasy' genres to explore family bonds and their unravellings. Spielberg has done it to a lesser or greater extent in a number of films; Shyamalan explores it not just in *The Sixth Sense*, but also *Unbreakable* and *Signs* (2002).

However, Shyamalan's comments are (perhaps deliberately) misleading. If there is a formula, it may be as much to do with working practices as the creative process. The fact that both directors have their films meticulously storyboarded before they start shooting means they both know exactly where they are going throughout the actual production process. There is perhaps an even more vital component to this formula, though. Spielberg and Shyamalan have learnt one very important aspect of editing: a film's pace should be determined by audience involvement, not temporal and rational constrictions. They

have both understood not just time but logic itself can go fly a kite as long as the spectator's emotions are being electrified.

Shyamalan once said, 'My hope is we broke so many rules we created a new rule'.[69] If he has done it with any of his films, he did it with this one.

NOTES:

69 Sourced from www.imdb.com

5. Institutions and the Star

The Sixth Sense opened in the US on the 6 August 1999 on 2,161 screens.[70] Forty weeks later, it was still the 56th most popular movie being seen by American cinema-going audiences, despite the fact it had been released on DVD and video by this time, before finally being withdrawn from exhibition.[71] By the end of its run, the film's US gross was $293,506,292 and the total world gross was $672,806,292. At $40 million,[72] it was a moderately budgeted Hollywood production at the time, bearing in mind a substantial part of it was Willis's salary (but see p.47). Three different production companies were involved in its development and the distribution rights were positively labyrinthine, involving more than ten distribution companies worldwide. As such, the development of this film as a business concern reflects the machinations of the Hollywood film industry.

Contemporary Hollywood is dominated by multinational conglomerates, which not only own the major studios, but also a range of other interests in the media and entertainment industries. As such, they can use these interests to support the films they produce, a process known as **synergy**. A conglomerate can produce a film, distribute it by selling or renting it to the exhibition circuit and indeed exhibit it in cinemas owned by them;[73] advertise the film in magazines and newspapers they produce and on radio and television stations they own; manufacture and sell the film merchandise through stores and shops they run; own the record label that releases the soundtrack. The vertical process of being involved at each stage of a film's journey from an idea to its projection onto the screen through production, distribution and exhibition, and the horizontal process of owning companies and media interests that can support the film in the marketplace is known as **vertical and horizontal integration**.

In the case of *The Sixth Sense*, vertical and horizontal integration played its part. The film was co-produced by Hollywood Pictures, a division of Walt Disney Studios, and distributed by Buena Vista and Buena Vista International, the studio's distribution arms at the time. It was promoted on the ABC television network as well as the ten local TV stations and numerous radio stations ABC owns. ABC is a subsidiary of the Walt Disney Company. It was also advertised on the A & E and Lifetime Entertainment cable and satellite channels, both of which Disney holds equity interests in. Disney also owns a number of other cable networks that may have advertised the film. Disney's publishing concerns at the time included Capitol City newspapers and an extensive range of magazines, some of which contained advertising for the film. It also owns Hyperion Books and several record labels, but none of these were utilised in respect to this film. However, had some executive decided that the film's ghosts might make a successful line of collectible figurines, no doubt they would have been stocked in Disney stores and appeared on the shelves at the theme parks.

Just weeks before the film started shooting, Joe Roth – Disney Studios' chief at the time – decided to offload total financing of the film by striking a deal with Spyglass Entertainment, a newly-created independent finance and production company headed by Roger Birnbaum (former head of Caravan Pictures) and Gary Barber (ex-vice chairman of Morgan Creek). Roth had not only worked with both of them previously, he had introduced them to each other. *The Sixth Sense* was the second film Spyglass Entertainment became financially involved in; the first was *Instinct* (1999), also a Disney product. However, due to its late signing on, Spyglass had virtually no input in the film creatively; this was done by The Kennedy/Marshall Company, who had bought the rights while affiliated to Disney[74] and who, amongst other things, suggested James Newton Howard to Shyamalan as a replacement for the original composer, a collaboration that has continued ever since.

NOTES:

70 While this date was primarily chosen in order to subliminally support public awareness of the film by linking the title to the release date, it fortuitously coincided with Shyamalan's birthday.

71 The initial US DVD/video release was on 28 March 2000; it remained on the theatrical circuit until 14 May 2000.

72 There is some disparity in respect to the film's costs. Shyamalan quoted two figures after finishing the film - $32 and $34 million. Many public domain sources state $55 million, but this almost certainly includes marketing costs. As such, I have selected the more considered figure of $40 million that has appeared in a lesser number of sources, but invariably with an additional $15 million marketing budget attached - resulting in the overall $55 million figure.

73 Though not wholly, as the 1948 Paramount Decree forbids a film studio from solely owning a theater chain in the US in order to ensure monopolisation does not occur.

74 The film's credits state it is a Kennedy/Marshall/Barry Mendel Production. Mendel was the producer who initially handled *The Sixth Sense* script.

5. Institutions and the Star

Spyglass did have an important role to play in terms of the film's success, though. Barber had constructed an international partnership structure in terms of distributing films globally. This meant that **The Sixth Sense**, while distributed through Disney's Buena Vista in the US and Buena Vista International in the UK, Australia, Latin America and Asia (excluding Japan), also had a substantial number of other distributors in place in other countries. Eureka, a large European acquisition alliance partnership between Kirch and Mediaset, owned the rights in Germany, Italy, Spain and Portugal, with Constantin Film having a theatrical sub-distribution deal with Eureka in Germany and Austria and Filmes Lusomundo having one in Portugal. Toho-Towa had the theatrical distribution rights to the film in Japan while Pony Canyon had the Japanese video rights. Svensk Filmindustri had all the Scandinavian rights except for pay-TV, which Canal Plus had along with all the rights in Belgium and non-theatrical rights in France, which were owned by Gaumont Buena Vista International (GBVI). Forum Film had the theatrical and video rights in Israel; Odeon had the rights in Greece; Gativideo had the Argentinian video rights.

This complicated distribution partnership with Spyglass Entertainment highlights an important aspect of Hollywood film-making today. World audiences are becoming increasingly important in terms of box-office returns and overseas distribution companies are increasingly financing Hollywood productions.[75] Birnbaum understood the specific ramifications of this when he said, in describing Spyglass Entertainment's agenda, 'The world is our marketplace and every decision we make, that one phase is before us. Every movie we make… is based upon how it will play around the world.'[76]

World audiences certainly had a financial impact in terms of **The Sixth Sense**. Over 56% of the film's total gross was achieved outside the US theatrical circuit. In Thailand it took $805,000 in the first five days; South Korea generated $870,000 and Singapore $680,000 in the first four and it became one of the ten biggest box-office opening successes in several countries, including Australia and Argentina. In the UK it grossed £257,479 in its opening weekend, despite being shown on only 9 screens (Buena Vista went for a limited release in this country, not done in the rest of Europe), going on to gross £4,972,499 million over the next seven days after it was exhibited on 430 screens and £25,407,279 million during its twenty week run. In Spain it racked up €26,556,344 and was seen 6,762,476 times (rather than people, bearing in mind an unknown number went twice or more). Even in the Netherlands, hardly one of the most populated countries in Europe, the film grossed €907,000 in its opening weekend (on 90 screens), generating €7,615,010 in total due to its 1,203,618 viewings. Germany must have been disappointing with only a $22,100,000 return.

It can be notoriously difficult to gather accurate figures in respect to a film's costs, both in terms of production and in terms of publicity and promotion, for a variety of reasons which space (and libel laws) forbids. However, it is clear, even though **The Sixth Sense**'s production costs have been quoted as ranging from $34 million to $55 million, the amount spent on marketing the film was significantly lower in terms of percentage costs than would be expected for a film of this budget. The commonly agreed estimate of **The Sixth Sense**'s marketing budget is $15 million; even when compared to the very lowest production figure, this works out at just over 44%, as opposed to the average marketing to production percentage of 49%. However, the most likely figure for the film's production costs is $40 million, which means the marketing budget was 37.5% of the production cost. While this figure is no small change, it does mean **The Sixth Sense** was seriously under-marketed in terms of the average Hollywood mainstream cinematic output.

The reasons for this are both manifest and manifold. They are manifest in that, once the box-office figures started to return, Disney's marketing department realised the job was being

---

NOTES:

75 On average, less than 20% of a film's total return now comes from the U.S. domestic box-office, though this percentage varies greatly depending on the type of film released.

76 Goodridge, *Screen International*, 1999.

done for them. Television, radio, print and theatrical advertising slots for **The Sixth Sense** in the US had been booked in advance and the publicity machine quickly understood to leave well enough alone. Great advertising, which at its best can result in the 'must see' factor, may place a film in the number one spot for the opening weekend; critical reviews may boost it; but **word-of-mouth** keeps a film there. **The Sixth Sense** became the second film in cinema history to gross over $20 million every weekend for five consecutive weeks, surpassed only by **Titanic** (1997). However, unlike the latter, there was no actor that appealed to teenage girls, no actress – semi-naked or otherwise – that appealed to teenage (and older) boys, no special effects that appealed to either, and both the love story and the action that dominate **Titanic** are secondary narratives in respect to the major motivations of the protagonists of **The Sixth Sense**.

To return to the film's US box-office history; rather than declining steadily, as occurs with the overwhelmingly majority of Hollywood film releases, **The Sixth Sense** actually rose in terms of percentage change no less than seven times during its 40 week theatrical run. In other words, the film made more money on a subsequent week than it did the previous one on seven occasions. One of these was during Labour Day weekend, another was over the New Year and a third was the weekend before Martin Luther King Day, an American public holiday always held on the third Monday of January. All these dates coincide with families and/or friends gathering together, igniting further word-of-mouth and corresponding outings to the cinema for a certain percentage of them. As for the other four occasions, three occurred the weeks before, during and after St. Valentine's Day, with the weekend before Valentine's Day showing a 273% rise in gross takings and the weekend after a further 73% increase. I will leave the reader to make(out) the connection. Only one week's rise seems to have no apparent cause for the film's increase in popularity other than it being shown on a wider number of screens that week, apart from the paradoxical reason of **The Sixth Sense**

being re-advertised at the time as an imminent DVD/video release.

Another factor that explains why the film was not given the standard marketing budget percentage was that to a certain extent Willis's presence was misleading. Though it meant **The Sixth Sense** was guaranteed to play in multiplexes and major theatres at a prime time of year, the distributors did not spend the usual amount that would be spent marketing a star-driven film because it was not star-driven. Audiences could potentially go to see the film and come out disappointed because their expectations (a Bruce Willis vehicle, with underlying assumptions of action) would not have been met, with corresponding negative feedback. This was why the advertising campaign did not 'sell' the film on the star's presence.

A further reason why the film's marketing budget was low is that obviously no one anticipated the film's phenomenal success. **The Sixth Sense** was a moderate budget production released in early August that Disney and Spyglass, while obviously hoping it would make a profit, certainly did not consider a blockbuster movie. Furthermore, the unexpected triumph of **The Blair Witch Project** no doubt undermined expectations of the film's financial return.

However, even taking all this into account, Buena Vista's promotion of the film was lacklustre, especially when it is considered that Shyamalan had constantly kept in mind how the film would be marketed while writing an unusual script:

> I tried to write very different pieces that don't feel like other movies. That's a great thing and a bad thing, because when they get to market they're lost. The studio doesn't know what it is, doesn't know which audience it's for... Writing **The Sixth Sense** was the first time I sat down and said, 'Now how are they going to sell this?' And I said, 'In the end I *think* they're going to sell it as classic, old-school horror.' So I said, 'I need

NOTES:

5. Institutions and the Star

to have enough of that in the movie for that [selling point] to be a legitimate representation of the movie…' I have to make sure when in doubt I'm always leaning there. 'Cause I gotta know what film I'm making, what audience I'm making it for…[77]

This approach was one of the major reasons why there had been such a feeding frenzy to buy the script. But while Shyamalan had carefully thought about how the film would be sold – 'Once I see how they can sell the story, then I can write it'[78] – apparently 'they' had trouble thinking in the same way. Shyamalan was aiming for a wide-ranging audience that liked intelligent horror films, rather than one specific demographic group, but if the marketing department were aware of this, they seem to have found such an audience a restriction in terms of selling a film. It is not that the marketing campaign was bad; rather that it was *vague*. And while it can be argued that, given such a wide remit, how else could they respond, they could have responded in a slightly better way than giving away one of the most important plot points in the film. The tagline 'I see dead people' is certainly effective, but it would have been a lot more effective had we not actually heard it *before* we saw the film. I'm no marketing executive, but it took me all of five seconds to think up 'Seeing is believing…?' or 'We all see what we want to see' and variations thereof as a better reflection of the film's content, if not also in terms of engendering audience interest.

Of course, there is a completely opposite opinion. Chris Pula – Disney's maverick head of publicity at the time (he is certainly not the epitome of 'team player') – considers the marketing campaign for **The Sixth Sense** to be one of his greatest successes and he is supported in this belief by Knowles, who wrote that the marketing of the film was 'as responsible as anything outside of the twist ending and word of mouth for its runaway success'.[79]

Whether the marketing division was or was not sure how to 'sell' the film, the release strategy showed no such doubts. The **release strategy** is decided on by the distributor/s, as they bear the cost of the film prints, an expensive process, and so carefully consider how many of these prints should be 'struck' in respect to the film's potential appeal. There are three basic types of release. One is the **platform** release, which is when a film is released in a limited amount of cinemas, usually in two or three cities, and then given a wider release across the country week by week. The idea behind this is to build audience anticipation, so that when the film does reach 'a cinema near you', you will already have heard about the film and want to see it – unless of course this does not occur, in which case the film is not given further release. The opposite of this is the wide or **saturation** release, when a film is released across thousands of screens simultaneously. This can be highly successful, as most films generate the majority of their box-office returns in the first week of each country. The third is the **limited** release, used for films where there is little expectation of commercial return but may generate specialised interest. These films are released in only one or two cinemas in major cities, usually in art house theatres, and will only gain further release (again invariably on the art house circuit) if the interest is confirmed, invariably through good reviews. However, there is a fourth type of release known as a **sleeper** release, which is different from the previous three in that it is audience rather than industry led. This is when a film is only released in a small number of cinemas, but generates a large amount of interest through positive word-of-mouth, as opposed to critical appreciation and marketing strategies. As a result, further prints are struck and the film gets a wider screening. A secondary outcome is that a sleeper release tends to run for a longer period of time on the theatrical circuit.

The Sixth Sense has been repeatedly described as a sleeper hit. However, this is not strictly speaking correct, for while it certainly shows sleeper tendencies in its success through word-of-mouth and its longevity in terms of remaining

NOTES:

77 Argent, ibid, 1999.

78 Quoted in Argent, ibid, 1999.

79 Knowles et al, *Ain't It Cool? Kicking Hollywood's Butt*, 2002.

on the theatrical circuit, it was given a saturation release. It opened on 2,161 screens for its first week and topped out at 2,821 screens by week nine. This shows an increase in release, but not an especially significant one for a successful saturation released film, particularly when it is considered that many of these prints would be shipped overseas in order to save on costs when the film opened months later in other countries, standard practice at the time.[80] *The Sixth Sense* was most certainly an unexpected hit, but only in terms of the amount of monies it generated; the thousands of prints initially struck clearly show a saturation release was always intended and that the film's US distributor believed it was going to be a financial success. Compare this to a genuine sleeper hit such as *The Blair Witch Project*, a small budget, independent film with a very limited initial release (27 screens on its opening weekend) that takes off (1,101 screens by its third weekend) and it can be seen that describing *The Sixth Sense* as a sleeper hit is somewhat a misnomer.

However, it is likely *The Blair Witch Project* would have been an even bigger sleeper hit had it not suffered to a certain extent from the release of *The Sixth Sense*. Shyamalan described his film as a 'dark, adult movie',[81] a description equally befitting the former. *The Blair Witch Project* was released mid-July, *The Sixth Sense* the second week in August. As both films appealed to the same audiences in the main, it was inevitable that one would lose attendance figures to the other. This turned out to be the case. Takings for *The Blair Witch Project* began declining rapidly after *The Sixth Sense* was released, despite there being very little difference between the number of screens showing each film for several weeks. The quirky, no-budget horror movie ended its run after nine weeks – and though it had made enormous profits (in terms of profit to cost ratio it is by far the most successful film made to date), there is little doubt it would have generated even more money had Shyamalan's film not jumped out of the shadows and gone 'boo'.

In her summary of contemporary Hollywood's approach to film as consumer product, Dawson states:

> Many factors – time of year, target audience, genre – will play a part in the reception of a film. Hollywood operates on the assumption that most films will lose money, but that the hits will reap big rewards.[82]

In so doing, she does not mention one other important factor: the **star**.

Definitions of the star abound. Sobchack and Sobchack, in differentiating between an actor and a star, described it thus: 'An actor or actress submerges his or her personality and creates a character; a star lets his or her own personality create the character.'[83] They go on to suggest that one of the reasons why audiences see films is to see stars 're-enact familiar personae', whereas actors 'do not stand out apart from their roles'. (They define a third type of actor as a 'screen performer' who 'occupy a middle ground between film actor and film star', such as Gene Hackman and Kevin Spacey.)[84] As such: 'This star quality has, in a sense, the same appeal and interest that the genre film has. There is the consistent, recognisable actor who varies only slightly from movie to movie.'[85] Ellis defines the star as 'at once ordinary and extraordinary, available for desire and yet unobtainable', going on to state that 'stars are presented both as stars and as ordinary people: as very special beings, and as being just like readers'.[86] Edgar Morin defined the star as a combination 'of filmic persona and off-screen personality' or 'actors with biographies'.[87] Allen and Gomery built on this, stating 'What the public knows... is not the star as person, but rather the star as image'.[88]

However, it is Dyer's consideration of the star that seems to be most prevalent at this time of writing. Though essentially a Marxist viewpoint, his analysis of the star and deconstruction of the star system is a valid one generally, in that it suggests a star's image is constructed in contemporary Hollywood in a similar way that a writer develops a character. Certain aspects are

---

NOTES:

80 No longer the case, due in part to the increased level of video and internet piracy. This has resulted in films now being exhibited around the world shortly after their U.S. release and even simultaneously on occasions - *Lord of the Rings: The Two Towers* (2002) being an example.

81 Nocenti, ibid, 2001.

82 Dawson, *Studying The Matrix*, 2003.

83 Sobchack and Sobchack, *An Introduction to Film*, 1987.

84 Sobchack and Sobchack, ibid, 1987.

85 Sobchack and Sobchack, ibid, 1987.

86 Ellis, *Visible Fictions: Cinema: Television: Video*, 1982.

87 Quoted in Allen and Gomery, *Film History: Theory and Practice*, 1985.

88 Allen and Robert, ibid, 1985.

consciously created while others happen by chance. In the author's case, this is known as 'inspiration' or 'the character taking over', i.e. an unexpected idea occurs in the process of writing that was never previously thought of (such as Shyamalan's crucial brainwave during his fifth draft of **The Sixth Sense** script that Crowe is dead). In the star's it can be anything from an unexpected public event (imagine how an action/adventure star's image would be enhanced and built on if they actually saved a drowning child in a sudden flash-flood) to a very private one (the world's most famous 'screen goddess' falling in love with a intellectual Jewish playwright will ring very loud bells for some readers, but even this might be surpassed if Julia Roberts actually did fall in love and marry a bookseller from Notting Hill or anywhere else for that matter).

Dyer considers the star as a construction through the amalgamation of four elements: promotion, publicity, films and criticism.

In terms of promotion, it is about what the producers of a film allow to be known in respect to the star's history; their origins and background, what led them to enter the acting profession, etc. In the days of the Hollywood Studio System, the 'star' apparently plucked from obscurity held an enormous appeal for the public and this still applies to a certain extent, in the same way fashion models do: it could be you if you dress right, look right, are beautiful/handsome or desirable, constantly monitor your weight/keep yourself muscularly trim and are spotted in the right place at the right time by the right person. However, tomorrow's potential stars have been informed in discrete, but no less uncertain, terms that they need more and/or other than this. You have to be talented, study your craft, work hard, keep on struggling and know others who are doing the same, hoping one of you will make the break. Today's stars have themselves intimated as much: Dustin Hoffman and Michael Douglas have both said this in one form or another in recent interviews.

Well, apparently not. Béatrice Dalle was cast in **37°2 le matin**, a.k.a. **Betty Blue** (1986), by Jean-Jacques Beineix because of her appearance on the cover of *Photo Revue* (used on the film poster), despite never having acted or even trained as such; Tom Cruise was forced to take on a larger role in **Taps** (1981) or else be fired because it was recognised he had star potential, despite his resistance to do so due to his dyslexia (the need to learn more lines); Bruce Willis wandered into the casting auditions for the TV series *Moonlighting* on the last day as an off-chance… or so the publicity machines would have us believe. And, lest we forget, Klinton Spilsbury was plucked from 'obscurity' to star in the big-budget film **The Legend of the Lone Ranger** (1981), never to be heard from again, supposedly because of his behaviour both on and off the set (the film's disastrous box-office performance having nothing to do with it, of course).

If outrageous behaviour can 'kill off' a star (in-the-making or otherwise), consider the off-set antics of Colin Farrell which began before, during and certainly after his first starring role in a Hollywood film (it once far exceeded the publicity machine but is now running in collaboration with it); let alone Hugh Grant, who not only transgressed the 'rules' but trampled all over them by being very publicly caught in a compromising situation with a prostitute. Yet Grant did not merely hold on to his status as one of the few major contemporary British Hollywood stars – and the only one along the lines of Cary Grant – he built on it.[89] This is where Dyer's second consideration of the star comes into play. Publicity – what is known about a star through newspaper articles, magazine gossip, radio and television spots, and interviews in general from *Sight and Sound* to *Horse and Hound* (sic) – is part of what constitutes and maintains that star's standing. However, this publicity is controlled, part-controlled or at least semi-colluded with by the industry.[90] Journalism now serves Hollywood, not the other way around; the same quotes and sound-bites appear repeatedly and the studio press-kits are used to launch articles and broadcasts. In doing so,

---

NOTES:

89 This is not merely a contemporary phenomenon. Roscoe 'Fatty' Arbuckle was destroyed as a star after the death of actress Virginia Rappe at a particularly wild party, whereas Charlie Chaplin continued despite the revelations of his penchant for young girls (see Kenneth Anger's *Hollywood Babylon*, New York: Dell, 1981, for all the salacious details).

90 When it is not, litigation is often threatened if not enacted (which in itself can be used to heighten a star's presence in the public eye).

though Dyer does not directly put it as such, publicity attempts to structure the star 'so that some meanings… are foregrounded and others masked or displaced'.[91] This is an intellectual way of saying 'withholding information' or 'damage limitation'. Stars can construct themselves through publicity as much as they are developed by the industry, but in doing so they are assisted by the publicity machine or at least have its tacit approval. 'Bad boys' become bad boys, for example, because the industry wants them to be seen as such. And when it does not, those bad boys have to change or adapt their image (Sean Penn) or risk finding themselves left out in the cold, with only a few eventually returning to the fold through others' willingness to take a chance on them (Dennis Hopper).

The third element Dyer considers helps to define a star is the films they appear in, in that the roles they play draw out the star's particular qualities. In effect, certain types of role are tailored to particular stars in the knowledge that the spectator will respond to their enactment of them in terms of box-office success. The majority of stars who reach that status do so because they consistently appear in a certain type of role the audience has responded to. However, once they become stars they can then exercise their power to move into other types of role. If they are successful they can shed the restrictive nature of being 'typecast'; if not they not only have to abandon their aspirations, they risk losing their star status. Tom Hanks successfully managed to manoeuvre himself from comic actor to dramatic, despite the seemingly inevitable lean period, and is now able to star in any number of different roles. Sylvester Stallone failed to do so (the commercial disaster of *F.I.S.T.* (1978) halted his development as a 'serious' dramatic actor and despite several attempts to make a diagonal shift into action comedy, he never succeeded) and his increasingly infrequent appearances on the screen have invariably been in the same type of role that made his name (*Cop Land* (1997) being an honourable semi-exception).

The last area Dyer pinpoints is that of criticism and commentary. In effect, this is the value of the star to the film industry in respect to how their work is critically considered and acclaimed. This critical appreciation is not limited to recognised film critics' reviews and evaluations, but also to those of film fans, buffs and geeks. The opinions of Roger Ebert,[92] Philip French, Barry Norman, David Thomson *et al.* may appear in the press and on television, but these opinions are increasingly becoming less important than those posted on aintitcoolnews.com, and the myriad other internet fan and film sites and chatrooms. To put it another way, Robert De Niro's performance in a film may be critically assessed in terms of acting ability, but Jackie Chan's latest starring role will be considered in quite a different context. It is how they are debated as a star, whether as an **actor**, a **screen presence** or a **professional stunt person**, that determines their currency or standing in the Hollywood film industry. It is highly unlikely Jackie Chan will ever win a Best Actor award for a dramatic role, but as long as he continues to perform impressive physical stunts (and to a lesser extent entertain the audience comically) in films that are financially successful he will remain a star, no matter how much his films are slated by professional critics. Marilyn Monroe, despite her best efforts, was never a great actress, but her screen presence is undeniable, which is why audiences constantly revisit her films, despite the fact some of them were not born until long after her death. Marlon Brando will always be considered a great actor, no matter the quality of the films he appeared in (and he certainly made some bad ones).

These sub-divisions of actor, screen presence and professional stunt-person actually reveal how few stars are considered as having more than one of these necessary attributes. There have been hundreds of stars during Hollywood's history, but only a number are still remembered or listed amongst the 'greats' – and the majority of them combine two of these three criteria. As for a star who displays all three… answers on a postcard please.

NOTES:

91 Dyer, *Stars*, 1979.

92 Who, incidentally, wrote the script for Russ Meyer's previously-mentioned *Beneath the Valley of the Ultra-Vixens*.

5. Institutions and the Star

Ultimately, though, the star is a finely balanced monetary equation. In the black column, they represent capital (their worth to the studio) and their value as an investment (the profit guaranteed by their appearance in a film); in the red is the outlay they require (their expense in terms of fees, incentives and percentage profits).

In the days of the Hollywood Studio System, the star was just another talent under contract. It could be an expensive contract certainly, but at the end of the day the star was committed to making a certain number of films in a certain period of time. It was the studio who had the final say in deciding what pictures the star would appear in, whether they would be lent out to other studios' projects or not and even – if Louis B. Mayer's alleged relationship with John Gilbert is anything to go by – whether they would continue to be a star at all. As far as the studio owners were concerned this was only right; they were footing the bills after all. In the 1950s, however, with the advent of television and other detrimental factors, times were getting tougher and the studios wanted someone else to share the risk. Stars were an obvious choice. As a result a new kind of deal was formed: instead of being paid completely up front, the star would work for a reduced salary but had a piece of the 'back end' in the form of net participation. In other words, if the film bombed, the studio did not have to foot such a large bill, but if it succeeded the star shared in the financial rewards.

Nowadays, this risk-sharing approach has become a no-risk approach. Major stars can not only demand an enormous up-front payment ($20–25 million is no longer uncommon for those stars in the very highest echelon) but their agents also negotiate high back end percentages both in respect of gross box-office receipts and in terms of profit participation in DVD/video, merchandising and other ancillary revenues. Furthermore, as the film crosses certain thresholds in terms of profits, the greater the percentage and payments the star gets. A star may even get a bonus for winning a best actor Oscar, something that will do their career no

harm in itself.[93] What all this means is that a star can now make a substantial amount of money no matter how badly the film performs and will make an even greater amount if it is a success. There is a downside, however. If they appear in several box-office failures in a row, their standing in respect to the A list (never mind the Triple A) is that they may no longer be on it.

Some stars weather the storm. John Travolta disappeared into Z-film territory[94] before his triumphant return in *Pulp Fiction*, *Get Shorty* (1995) and *Broken Arrow* (1996) resulted in him again becoming one of the highest-paid stars in the industry. Others do not. Mickey Rourke has never managed to return to grace after several unsuccessful releases and now appears on the whole in low budget independent films, in which he consistently repeats his stock-in-trade role of the potentially dangerous misfit outsider, though *Sin City* (2005) may finally prove to be his reversal of fortune. Bruce Willis, however, is one of those male stars who seems to walk that fine line between 'untouchable' (Tom Cruise, Jim Carrey, Jack Nicholson) and 'untouched' (Tom Selleck, Steve Guttenberg, Don Johnson)[95], and his signing to *The Sixth Sense* is a fascinating and intricate example of the deals that occur in contemporary Hollywood in terms of the studios' relationships with the stars.

Willis's cinematic career has certainly had its ups and downs. Hits such as the *Die Hard* trilogy (1988, 1990, 1995) and *Pulp Fiction* have been more than balanced out by some very expensive flops (*The Bonfire of the Vanities* (1990), *Hudson Hawk* (1991) and *Last Man Standing* (1996) to name but three) and in 1997 he found himself in an unenviable position. Of the last four films he had starred in, only one, *The Fifth Element* (1997), had been a resounding success and he knew the already-recognised-within-the-industry disaster of *Mercury Rising* was still waiting in the wings. Moreover, several weeks into the filming of *Broadway Brawler*, which he was producing as well as starring in, the original director had been fired, the replacement was struggling and Willis was convinced the project

NOTES:

93 On the other hand, winning one of the top five awards (best film, director, actor, actress and surprisingly - given how low writers come in the Hollywood pecking order - screenplay) can generate up to ten times the amount of box-office receipts a film would otherwise get.

94 *Perfect* (1985) surely contains one of the most cringe-worthy sequences in recent cinematic history.

95 He has been described as 'Part-Time Boxoffice Magnet/Full-Time Smark Aleck… His great strength: his on-screen presence as an Everyman coping with events beyond the ken of normal humanity.' (Parsons, *Cinefantastique*, 2001.)

was doomed to failure. The actor no longer wanted to continue with the film, but to walk away from it was going to be expensive. Arnold Rifkin, Willis's agent and president of the William Morris Agency at the time, calculated it would cost the star $12 million to close the production down. So Rifkin contacted Joe Roth to make a deal: if Disney paid off the **Broadway Brawler** costs, Willis would give them a three-picture commitment in exchange.

In doing so, Willis granted the studio a number of important concessions. Firstly, he would work on each film for a reduced per-film wage of $15 million. Secondly, the costs of **Broadway Brawler** would be repaid over the course of the three films (as **Broadway Brawler**'s shutdown costs eventually exceeded $17 million, this resulted in approximately $6 million of each fee being returned to Disney). Thirdly, Willis would waive his 15%+ gross profit cut from the first film.

Roth agreed to the deal. He did so not just out of magnanimity or to keep Rifkin – head of arguably the most powerful film agency at the time – sweet, but because he too was in a difficult position. **Armageddon** was nearing its start date and Disney was in the process of casting, but they were up against competition. DreamWorks were ahead of them with a similarly themed film, **Deep Impact** (1998), which would be released first. However, **Deep Impact**, with Morgan Freeman and Téa Leoni, did not have a globally recognised star and Roth thought this was a sure way to distinguish his film from its competitor. Willis was an ideal choice. As Roth himself said, 'I started to get worried… And then I got Arnold's [Rifkin's] call'.[96]

Armageddon was the biggest grossing film of 1998 – and as Disney did not have to pay Willis his standard gross-profit deal, which would have amounted to around $45 million on the theatrical release alone, they not only recouped their payout on **Broadway Brawler** from just his first film with them, they were ahead of the game.

While **Armageddon** was still in production Disney set about looking for another strong action picture for Willis, but in vain. Though the star had essentially been shoe-horned into one film did not mean he was going to commit to just anything, just as the studio were not going to say yes to any project he wanted to do. Then Carl Waynberg, a young agent at William Morris, read the screenplay for **The Sixth Sense** that Disney had purchased and thought it was a great part for Willis. He persuaded Rifkin to do the same, using the tried and tested formula of offering to be fired if Rifkin didn't agree with him (how many agents have actually been 'let go' when the boss did not concur?). Waynberg kept his job, Rifkin passed the script onto Willis, who read it and then requested to see **Wide Awake**. As he was filming **Armageddon** at the time, it took him a while to respond, but when it came (after watching a film in which a child sets out to find God, possibly not the best calling card for a young director to a major star whose own calling card was as an action hero), the response was not only positive, it was definite. Willis committed, saying 'This kid knows what he's doing'.[97] As Waynberg had surmised and Shyamalan was also aware of, the role of Crowe needed a 'superstar who was hungry – who had something to prove'.[98] Rifkin spoke to Roth and the intended low-budget $10 million film (which *was* low-budget as far as Disney was concerned; especially as $3 million had already been pledged to Shyamalan alone) became something very different indeed.

While no one would suggest that Willis is the sole reason why **The Sixth Sense** was such a huge success, the fact it was such a phenomenal money-maker re-affirmed the actor's status as one of contemporary Hollywood's most 'bankable' stars. It also placed Shyamalan firmly on the cinematic map. Despite refusing to move to Hollywood and continuing to write spec scripts rather than signing a deal with a studio, he has consistently ranked in the top 30 of Premiere's annual Power 100 list ever since, with increasing up-front and deferred payments as a result ($3 million for **The Sixth Sense**; $10 million for

Fig. 13: Bruce Willis in **Die Hard**: from action hero...

NOTES:

96 Horn, *Premiere*, 2000.

97 Quoted in Argent, ibid, 1999.

98 Horn, ibid, 2000.

5. Institutions and the Star

Fig. 14: ...to Mr Zero

movie story, deal with B-movie subjects, and I treat it as if it's an A-movie in terms of my approach, my crew, my actors, my ethics and so on. I guess that's my trademark…'[101] Reportedly, if the film posters in his office are anything to go by (and they are), three of his favourite films are *Die Hard, Raiders of the Lost Ark* and *The Exorcist*. All these films were B-movies plots – a heist that goes wrong, a 'boys' own' adventure story straight from the pulps and a tale of demonic possession – given the A-movie treatment, and all of them were commercial blockbusters, loved by audiences and admired by critics (either at the time or retrospectively acknowledged). Shyamalan set out to do the same with *The Sixth Sense*.

He succeeded.

Unbreakable; $12.5 million for *Signs*). The reality is *The Sixth Sense* was a success due to cinema-goers responding to it so strongly and telling others about it, but no-one involved in the film suffered as a result.

In Hollywood, everybody wins when they are involved in a success. It is what they do after that counts. Willis used Disney's distribution's arm to release his adaptation of Kurt Vonnegut's *Breakfast of Champions* (1999), a critical and commercial failure that earned a mere $175,370 at the US box-office, and has since returned to the hit-and-miss approach. Shyamalan, however, continued to write and direct films in the way he wanted to do them.

Shyamalan has said 'it's my job to make money for the studio'[99] and 'I'm not making pictures for that [commercial] six week period, I'm making movies for ten years from now'.[100] These statements show his desire to be two things: a commercially successful director and an auteur. *The Sixth Sense* shows both these desires at work through its narrative development and stylistic approach. You just have to recognise the signs (sic).

However, if there is a single quote that sums up Shyamalan's method of film-making, it is perhaps this one: 'I think I take what you might call a B-

NOTES:

99 Sourced from www.imdb.com

100 tiscali.co.uk/entertainment/broadband/the village/interview.html

101 Sourced from www.imdb.com

Conclusion

The Sixth Sense is not a perfect film in terms of logical consistency. There are discrepancies in its narrative you could drive a proverbial truck through, with space on either side. Here are just a few. Malcolm may only see what he wants to see, but he must have wondered why no one converses with him or even acknowledges his presence apart from Cole and (in a negative way) Anna. He changes clothes twice in the film; even if he is dead he could hardly fail to notice the bloody hole in his back, particularly as all the other ghosts in the film seem to be aware of how they died. How does Malcolm get hold of Cole's case history? Why does Malcolm not question Anna about the possibility of her having an affair, considering that Sean blatantly turns up at the house and is seen by Malcolm leaving it one night? Malcolm uses the basement as his study, but before he died it seems to have been used only to store wine. As such, why does he start working there after he is dead rather than continue where he did before? (Is there another basement room? How many Philadelphian town houses have two basements!) If the temperature drops when a ghost is present, why does no one show signs of being cold at Kyra's funeral, especially as there are two ghosts in attendance at the time? Lynn has pictures of Cole hanging on the wall, which she either had framed or framed herself, yet she never noticed the strange lights that appear in them before? There are others, including the most obvious discrepancy, but I will leave the rest for you to discover.

Shyamalan is a meticulous scriptwriter. He could have built reasonable visual or verbal explanations why all of the above occur in terms of the film's verisimilitude. However, in doing so, the point of the film would have been lost. *The Sixth Sense* is not primarily concerned with narrative holes and the filling of them, but rather narrative *effect*. This is not an Agatha Christie or Colin Dexter mystery where all the loose ends are summarily tied up and nothing is left in doubt. It is a different type of investigation where discrepancies exist, but they are unimportant as long as the reason why it is being undertaken is recognised and understood by the spectator. *The Sixth Sense* may be a puzzle, but it is a puzzle that is only concerned with delivering the idea of the picture. It does not matter that every piece does not fit; it matters even less that some pieces will never fit. As long as the audience receive the message, find the resolution emotionally satisfying and the film in general thoughtful, the fact that some aspects of it are not clearly explained fully is of little concern. *The Sixth Sense* is, in its own way, the cinematic equivalent of Monet's Giverny pictures, not the Photorealist paintings of Robert Cottingham or Richard Estes.

Of course, Shyamalan's film is not a painting but a moving picture. There is not a single frame that is a perfectly balanced composition, not one image that could be considered truly beautiful or sublime in its own right. It is nearer to Warhol's approach than Vermeer's, but it contains elements of both. There is substance as well as surface. There is depth here. At the end of the day – beyond the deals, the statistics, the revenues, the narrative and genre intricacies – it does contain meaning.

You just have to want to see.

NOTES:

Classroom Worksheets
Narrative

Classical Hollywood narrative invariably has a three-act structure with a cause–effect pattern (one action or event results in another, which leads to another, etc.).

Task

Apply this three-act structure to *The Sixth Sense*:

1   What is the **exposition** (beginning), the **development** (middle) and the **resolution** (end) of the film in your opinion? (Hint: Consider that every **protagonist** (character) within the film may have a different start and end point. How many resolutions are there in respect to each and when they do they occur?)

2   Where do you think each 'act' ends and the other begins?

3   Is the beginning of the film the same as its introduction? If not, how does it differ?

4   Could the film be considered unusual in terms of a three-act structure? If so, why? Does any part of it appear to be unusually long?

5   Who is the dominant protagonist in *The Sixth Sense* in terms of the film's narrative?

Tzvetan Todorov developed the idea of narrative circularity in terms of equilibrium, disequilibrium and new equilibrium. When Todorov's approach is applied to *The Sixth Sense*:

6   Is it undermined in any way in the narrative development of the film?

7   Is the resolution of the film actually a resolution? How is a new equilibrium achieved considering Malcolm discovers he is dead? What exactly has been resolved?

Task

How many plot-holes are there within the film? In groups, write down as many as you can think of. In terms of its narrative, is the film weakened by them? Do they actually matter at all?

Discussion

Why do you think *The Sixth Sense* was so successful? After all, it was not the first film to have an unexpected twist at the end. What made this film so popular?

Task

What is a 'paradigm shift'? Find out the meaning and then apply it to the narrative of *The Sixth Sense*. Does it help in terms of your understanding of the film's popularity?

Genre

Genre is a way of classifying films in terms of iconography, stylistic approaches and particular narrative considerations. In other words, it helps the spectator to identify similarities between one film and another in terms of what they appreciate and enjoy. As such, it assists audiences in choosing what films they would like to see.

Discussion

The Sixth Sense has been described as both a 'psychological horror' and a 'supernatural thriller'. What do you consider to be the difference between the two descriptions?

Task

Compare and contrast *The Sixth Sense* in respect to the following psychological horror/supernatural thriller films:

	Similarities	Differences
The Blair Witch Project (1999)		
The Others (2001)		
The Shining (1980)		

Now compare it to the following films:

	Similarities	Differences
Les Diaboliques (1955)		
House of Games (1987)		
Raiders of the Lost Ark (1981)		

In your opinion, are there more similarities between *The Sixth Sense* and the first set of films or the second? What does this tell you in respect to both this film and genre films in general?

Discussion

Apart from horror and suspense, what other genre aspects appear within the film? Do you agree it is a maturation (coming-of-age) film and a love story? If so, why? What other genres and sub-genres can you identify within the film?

Themes

In music there is the idea of the 'contrapuntal theme' – in that the style of the song contradicts the narrative lyrics (imagine a country and western song about the problems of living in an inner-city ghetto).

Discussion

Does the style of *The Sixth Sense* contradict its themes?

Task

In groups, identify the themes in *The Sixth Sense*. Draw up a list and then nominate the most important to the class:

1   Did you identify five? If not, consider that the film perhaps does not contain that many or does not convey them clearly.

2   If you had to narrow your choice down to three in terms of thematic importance, which themes would you choose?

Discussion

In your opinion, what is the major theme of *The Sixth Sense*? Give reasons for your decision.

Film Language

Task

Research the conventions of **classical continuity editing** and then consider the following:

1 Which of these conventions are not used in *The Sixth Sense* and why?

2 Are any of these conventions used in an unusual way in respect to the majority of Hollywood output? Again, why?

Discussion

The colour **red** predominantly appears in the film. In groups, consider why this colour was used and what does it represent or signify? After comparing your conclusions with others in the class, how many did you see, how many did you miss and how many do you now recall? How does the *mise-en-scène* emphasise this colour (think about the colours surrounding it whenever it appears)? Do you consider any of them to be unusual in terms of the events occurring at the time?

Task

The Sixth Sense is set in the American city of **Philadelphia**. Research into why the film was set in this particular city. Do you think the film could have been filmed anywhere else (it does not have to be in America)? If so, why?

Task

As a class, split into two groups. One group should come up with reasons why *The Sixth Sense* is an 'old fashioned' horror film in respect to the **special effects**; the other should consider how it uses contemporary special effects. Compare the two.

Task

If you have seen any other M. Night Shyamalan films (currently **Praying With Anger, Wide Awake, Unbreakable, Signs, The Village** and, in 2006, **The Lady in the Lake**), what consistencies have you noticed in respect to these films and *The Sixth Sense* in terms of film language (or any other aspects)? After considering this, go to www.imdb.com/name/nm0796117/bio and see what is written there (do not necessarily disregard your own conclusions).

Discussion

Is *The Sixth Sense* a 'star-driven' film? How many sequences occur where Bruce Willis is not present? Does the number matter?

Discussion

The Sixth Sense is one of the most financially successful films ever made. Consider why there has been no sequel.

Task

Write a 200 word synopsis of *The Sixth Sense 2*. Include the ending (it does not have to be a surprise twist).

Task

In the US, *The Sixth Sense* was shown on 2161 screens on its opening weekend; in the UK it was shown on 9. Research the different types of **release strategy** and decide what strategy was used for the film in each country. Why do you think they were so different?

Task

By studying the statistics opposite, it can be seen that the *The Sixth Sense* rose seven times in box-office popularity in the US during its cinematic exhibition (emphasised in bold). Why? (Hint: Consider there may be important dates in the US that do not occur in the UK.)

The Sixth Sense

Week	Weekend Gross	Theaters	Thr. Avg	Total	Rank	% Change
Aug 6-8	$26.681	2,161	$12,347	$26.681	1	NEW
Aug 13-15	$25.765	2,395	$10.758	$69.662	1	–3%
Aug 20-22	$23.950	2,688	$8,910	$107.506	1	–7%
Aug 27-29	$20.099	2,763	$7,274	$138.854	1	–16%
Sep 3-6	$29.217	2,775	$10,529	$176.245	1	**+45%**
Sep 10-12	$16.511	2,782	$5,935	$197.665	2	–28%
Sep 17-19	$11.207	2,788	$4,020	$213.276	3	–32%
Sep 24-26	$8.435	2,791	$3,022	$225.042	3	–25%
Oct 1-3	$7.025	2,821	$2,490	$234.548	5	–17%
Oct 8-10	$6.124	2,784	$2,200	$242.710	6	–13%
Oct 15-17	$5.160	2,682	$1,924	$249.858	8	–16%
Oct 22-24	$4.058	2,191	$1,852	$255.501	10	–21%
Oct 29-31	$3.201	2,051	$1,561	$259.836	8	–21%
Nov 5-7	$3.132	1,802	$1,738	$264.043	8	–2%
Nov 12-14	$2.563	1,418	$1,807	$267.742	10	–18%
Nov 19-21	$1.615	1,219	$1,325	$269.976	11	–37%
Nov 26-28	$1.543	1,017	$1,517	$272.319	12	–4%
Dec 3-5	$0.967	1,034	$935	$273.550	12	–37%
Dec 10-12	$0.667	856	$779	$274.478	12	–31%
Dec 17-19	$0.492	623	$789	$275.177	15	–26%
Dec 24-26	$0.213	361	$590	$275.718	23	–57%
Dec 31-Jan 2	$0.342	267	$1,282	$276.386	22	**+61%**
Jan 7-9	$0.332	255	$1,304	$276.863	25	–3%
Jan 14-17	$0.416	237	$1,753	$277.400	27	**+25%**
Jan 21-23	$0.248	223	$1,111	$277.709	34	–40%
Jan 28-30	$0.236	220	$1,072	$278.016	33	–5%
Feb 4-6	$0.299	220	$1,359	$278.387	32	**+27%**
Feb 11-13	$1.116	831	$1,343	$279.575	17	**+273%**
Feb 18-21	$1.934	894	$2,163	$282.006	16	**+73%**
Feb 25-27	$1.548	992	$1,560	$283.918	15	–20%
Mar 3-5	$1.193	759	$1,572	$285.520	19	–23%
Mar 10-12	$0.968	672	$1,440	$286.827	20	–19%
Mar 17-19	$1.281	878	$1,459	$288.477	16	**+32%**
Mar 24-26	$1.280	876	$1,462	$290.288	13	0%
Mar 31-Apr 2	$0.902	722	$1,250	$291.746	17	–30%
Apr 7-9	$0.513	579	$886	$292.516	20	–43%
Apr 14-16	$0.272	450	$605	$292.934	24	–47%
Apr 21-23	$0.162	323	$500	$293.244	30	–41%
Apr 28-30	$0.084	211	$399	$293.414	42	–48%
May 5-7	$0.036	91	$395	$293.477	56	–57%

Source: www.the-movie-times.com.

THE 1999 WORLDWIDE BOX OFFICE TOP TEN

Look at the table below, detailing the top films of 1999.

	Film	Budget (US)	Release Date	Total Gross
1	*Star Wars Episode I: The Phantom Menace*	$115m	19 May	$923.0m
2	*The Sixth Sense*	$55m	6 Aug	$661.5m
3	*Toy Story 2*	$90m	24 Nov	$485.7m
4	*The Matrix*	$65m	31 Mar	$456.4m
5	*Tarzan*	$150m	18 Jun	$435.3m
6	*The Mummy*	$76m	5 Jul	$413.3m
7	*Notting Hill*	$42m	28 May	$363.1m
8	*The World is Not Enough*	$120m	19 Nov	$352.0m
9	*American Beauty*	$15m	17 Sep	$336.1m
10	*Austin Powers: The Spy Who Shagged Me*	$33m	11 Jun	$310.3m

Source: www.boxofficereport.com [adapted].

In your opinion, what are the films' **genres**? Which demographic audience (a single group of people in terms of age, gender, race, etc.) do you think they are primarily aimed at?

How many of them do you consider to be sequels? Consider sequels in respect to audiences and film budgets. Why do Hollywood studios spend money on sequels rather than making 'original' films? Research into whether this a contemporary Hollywood approach. What was the first Hollywood sequel?

Is *The Sixth Sense* similar in terms of **genre** to any other film in the Top Ten?

Look at the times of year each film was released. Are there any patterns that you can see? (For example, how many films were released in the run up to Christmas? Are there any seasonal patterns?) Compare *The Sixth Sense* with respect to the release of the other films. What conclusion(s) can you make?

Consider each film's negative costs and gross profits (in other words, how much did each film cost to make and how much did it earn). What were the most successful films in your opinion?

What do you think the term 'sleeper hit' (a.k.a. sleeper release) means? Find out if your interpretation is a correct one. Which films in the Top Ten do you consider to be sleeper releases? Why do you think they were so successful?

AND FINALLY, JUST FOR FUN

What do you consider to be the biggest plot-hole in *The Sixth Sense* and why?

(The answer is so obvious it is invariably missed. Until he understands and accepts his 'gift', Cole's breath always becomes cold when the film's ghosts get up close and personal in their need to communicate with him ... except when he first meets Malcolm. The argument that Cole does not do this because Malcolm is unaware he is dead is fallacious. In this film, the *mise-en-scéne* clearly sets up the idea that the temperature drops when a ghost is present; whether the ghost is aware of their state or not is immaterial. Students often conclude through class discussion that the biggest discrepancy is Malcolm's breaking of the glass, which he cannot do due to his inability to affect physical objects. However, we do not directly see Malcolm doing this. As to what else may have caused it, how about a confused bird or a pebble ricocheting from the tyres of a passing car? Your guess is as good as mine.)

Filmography/Bibliography

Filmography

The Sixth Sense (1999), 2 Disc Collector's Edition DVD released by Hollywood Pictures Home Video and Spyglass Entertainment, 2002.

Unbreakable (2000), 2 Disc Collector's Edition DVD released by Touchstone Home Video, 2001.

Signs (2002), DVD released by Touchstone Home Entertainment, 2003.

The Village (2004), DVD released by Touchstone Home Entertainment, 2005.

Bibliography

Allen, Robert and Gomery, Douglas, *Film History: Theory and Practice*, New York: Alfred Knopf, 1985.

Bart, Peter and Guber, Peter, *Shoot Out: Surviving Fame and [Mis]Fortune in Hollywood*, London: Faber and Faber, 2003.

Bordwell, David and Thompson, Kristin, *Film Art: An Introduction (Sixth Edition)*, New York: McGraw-Hill, 2002.

Buckland, Warren, *Film Studies*, London: Hodder & Stoughton Teach Yourself Books, 1998.

Dawson, Anna, *Studying The Matrix*, Leighton Buzzard: Auteur, 2003.

Dyer, Richard, *Stars*, London: BFI, 1979.

Ellis, John, *Visible Fictions: Cinema: Television: Video*, London: Routledge & Kegan Paul, 1982.

Gilbey, Ryan, *It Don't Worry Me*, London: Faber and Faber, 2003.

Goldman, William, *Adventures in the Screen Trade*, New York: Warner Books, 1983.

Hayward, Susan, *Cinema Studies: The Key Concepts (Second Edition)*, London and New York: Routledge, 2000.

Lehman, Peter and Luhr, William, *Thinking About Movies: Watching, Questioning, Enjoying (Second Edition)*, Oxford: Blackwell, 2003.

Jancovich, Mark, *Horror*, London: Batsford, 1992.

Knowles, Harry, Cullum, Paul and Ebner, Mark, *Ain't It Cool? Kicking Hollywood's Butt*, London: Boxtree, 2002 (published as *Ain't It Cool? Hollywood's Redheaded Stepchild Speaks Out*, New York: Warner, 2002).

Maltby, Richard, *Hollywood Cinema (Second Edition)*, Oxford: Blackwell, 2003.

McKee, Robert, *Story*, New York: Regan Books, 1997.

Redmond, Sean, *Studying Blade Runner*, Leighton Buzzard: Auteur, 2003.

Scarratt, Elaine, *Science Fiction Film: A Teacher's Guide to the Genre*, Leighton Buzzard: Auteur, 2001.

Sobchack, Thomas and Sobchack, Vivien, *An Introduction to Film (Second Edition)*, London: Longman, 1987.

Strinati, Dominic, *An Introduction to Studying Popular Culture*, London and New York: Routledge, 2000.

Todorov, Tzvetan, *The Fantastic: A Structural Approach to a Literal Concept*, Cleveland and London: Case Western Reserve University Press, 1973.

NOTES:

Articles

Argent, Daniel, 'The Sixth Sense', Creative Screenwriting, Vol. 6, No. 5, Sept./Oct. 1999, pp. 38–46.

Bernstein, Jill, 'The Education of M. Night Shyamalan', Premiere, Nov. 2000, pp. 57-60.

Clarke, Roger, 'Will this Man be the New Spielberg?', Evening Standard, 4 Nov. 1999, p. 33.

Curtis, Quentin, 'Young Gun with the Spielberg Touch', Daily Telegraph, 29 Oct.1999, p. 23.

D'Antonio, Michael, 'The Unguarded Heart: The Uncommon Sense of M. Night Shyamalan', Written By, March 2000, pp. 16-23.

Goodridge, Mike, 'Spyglass: Making Dollars and Sense', Screen International, 29 Oct. 1999, pp. 12-13.

Harty, Kevin, 'Looking for Arthur in all the wrong places: a note on M. Night Shyamalan's The Sixth Sense', Arthuriana, Vol. 10, Issue 4, Winter 2000, pp. 58-62.

Holben, Jay, 'Impeccable Images', American Cinematographer, Vol. 81, No. 6, June 2000, pp. 82-86.

Horn, John, 'Triumph of the Willis', Premiere, Jan. 2000, pp. 35-36.

Mars-Jones, Adam, 'Death's Too Good For Them', The Times, 4 Nov. 1999, p. 46.

Nayman, Ira, 'The Man Who Wasn't There: Narrative Ambiguity in 3 Recent Hollywood Films', Creative Screenwriting, Vol. 8, No. 2, Mar./Apr. 2001, pp. 57-60.

Nocenti, Annie, 'Writing and Directing The Sixth Sense: A Talk with M. Night Shyamalan', Scenario, Vol. 5, No. 4, 2001, pp. 51-57, 184-187.

Parsons, Dan, 'Sci-Fi, Horror and Fantasy Films Power 2000' Cinefantastique, Vol. 32, No. 6, Feb. 2001, p.36.

Smith, Adam, 'Empireoneonone', Empire, Feb. 2001, pp. 99-101.

Strick, Philip, 'The Sixth Sense', Sight and Sound, Vol. 9, Issue 11, November 1999, p. 55.

Websites

www.boxofficereport.com
www.the-movie-times.com

Two sites showing box-office takings and statistics in a variety of ways.

www.camre.ac.uk/learning/7914/stars.htm

John White's summarised consideration of the 'star', including quotations from a range of texts.

www.imdb.com

The internet movie database is a comprehensive one-stop shop in respect to film in general.

tiscali.co.uk/entertainment/broadband/the village/interview.html

Video recording of an audience with M. Night Shyamalan held at The Ritzy, Brixton on 9 August 2004.

NOTES: